CLASSROOM DESIGN FOR STUDENT AGENCY

Create Spaces to Empower Young Readers and Writers

Classroom Design for Student Agency

Create Spaces to Empower Young Readers and Writers

Lynsey Burkins

Franki Sibberson

National Council of Teachers of English

Staff Editor: Cynthia Gomez
Manuscript Editor: Cynthia Gomez
Interior Design: Cynthia Gomez
Cover Design: Adrian Morgan
Cover Image: Marvin Young

ISBN: 978-0-8141-0155-1 (paperback); 978-0-8141-0156-8 (epub); 978-0-8141-0157-5 (PDF)

It is the policy of NCTE in its journals and other publications to provide a forum for the open discussion of ideas concerning the content and the teaching of English and the language arts. Publicity accorded to any particular point of view does not imply endorsement by the Executive Committee, the Board of Directors, or the membership at large, except in announcements of policy, where such endorsement is clearly specified.

NCTE provides equal employment opportunity to all staff members and applicants for employment without regard to race, color, religion, sex, national origin, age, physical, mental or perceived handicap/disability, sexual orientation including gender identity or expression, ancestry, genetic information, marital status, military status, unfavorable discharge from military service, pregnancy, citizenship status, personal appearance, matriculation or political affiliation, or any other protected status under applicable federal, state, and local laws.

Every effort has been made to provide current URLs and email addresses, but, because of the rapidly changing nature of the web, some sites and addresses may no longer be accessible.

Library of Congress Control Number: 2023940792

Contents

Foreword

By Carla Shalaby

For three years, I had the opportunity to participate in a design team working to renovate two historic buildings in schools suitable for serving the needs of elementary and high school students here in Detroit. Our team included architects, builders, interior designers, scholars specializing in movement, central office administrators, and educators. We debated everything: the paint colors and flooring materials; whether cubbies and coat hooks should be placed in the hallways or inside the classrooms; whether to create a maker-space or a more traditional art room; whether administrator offices should be placed together or spread around the buildings.

Questions about and arguments over power routinely surfaced during these conversations, because debates over seemingly simple design questions were deeply entangled in questions about our values, the messages we wanted to communicate, and what kind of school community we wanted to build.

Should the principal's office have a traditional desk, or a circular table? When meeting with families and children, would we want the principal facing opposite or seated adjacent to these others? Where should special education classrooms — too often relegated to far-off corners or basement classrooms — be located to signal inclusion? Where could single-stall bathrooms be placed to accommodate all genders and community members with privacy concerns, without hiding them away in places that people would have trouble reaching? Should kindergarten classrooms have individual desks or group tables? What kind of pedagogical choices would be available in one model or the other? Should the rooms housing books be called libraries? Reading rooms? Media centers? Quiet areas? Healing spaces? What colors signaled the kind of calm and peace we wanted children to experience? Could high schoolers be trusted with hidden-away comfy seating in some common area nooks and locker pods? If we intentionally built "calm corners" into each elementary classroom, would children pursue them as voluntary spaces of healing or would teachers use them as places for exclusionary time-outs?

Every design decision was a question of ethics, values, pedagogical communication, inclusion and exclusion, power and agency, teacher authority and children's rights, fairness and equity, justice and care. Yet, despite my nearly 20 years of working at the intersections of teaching and justice, I am ashamed to admit that this recent experience was my first time thinking deeply about the incredible importance of every single one of these design decisions.

What I wouldn't give to reverse time and instead begin my teaching career with this book in hand! Not only does this work awaken our consciousness to the entangled relationships between and among agency, power, freedom, and design; it also concretely guides readers toward practical decision-making about the kinds of designs that best support and signal to children that they are free. That they are important. That they have choices. That they have rights and responsibilities. That they are readers and writers and thinkers and community members and most of all, that they are human beings. Lynsey and Franki walk us through the design of spaces with learner agency in mind, and in doing so, help us to envision and then build — together alongside our students — the kinds of classrooms that signal care, value, freedom, and mattering.

This gem of a resource is the clear, practical, beautiful, inspiring guide I wish I had as a classroom teacher, but am deeply grateful to have now as a human being deeply committed to creating spaces of learning in which children get the chance to practice their freedom ethically, responsibly, and wisely. The authors offer both nonnegotiables and spaces for discretion and debate; guiding principles that help us each to declare our values; firsthand stories of these principles in action; and resources to help cultivate the kinds of spaces our children deserve. Every educator, both experienced and brand new, will benefit tremendously from this rich and robust book. I am deeply grateful to Lynsey and Franki for writing it.

For those of us committed to trading our classroom models of control and compliance for opportunities to learn and practice freedom and care, let us begin by recognizing that we teach in and through every decision we make — not just in and through our lesson plans. The way we manage our classrooms — and as Franki and Lynsey remind us, the way we design our classrooms — is itself a curriculum teaching lessons about power, about choice, about freedom, and about the worth, value, and rights of young people in school.

Introduction to Classroom Design

There is nothing like welcoming a new group of students to a new school year. We love putting the final touches on our classrooms before children arrive in the fall. We have learned that this work is much more than about creating a cute and comfortable environment for children. The design decisions we make will impact learning across the coming year.

> *The deliberate design of learning environments requires an understanding of the full range of modalities of learning, not just the established modalities. Powerful design is expansive rather than exclusive in its focus, accommodating the full range of ways in which humans engage in deliberate learning. Design is about expanding rather than containing learning, opening access rather than controlling access, adapting to differences in learning modalities and preferences rather than restricting modalities and controlling preferences.*
>
> — Language of School Design

We both have moved into new homes recently. As much as we don't love the stress of moving, we love imagining a new space and all its possibilities. We love to create a space that we know will be perfect for everyone in our immediate family — the people who will live there.

We get this same feeling each summer as we ready our classrooms for a new school year. We love the preparation that we do as we prepare to welcome a new group of children. We love a cute room, but our goal is to make sure we create a space where every child feels welcome, a space where students

We want space for the whole class to gather for learning.

can see themselves being part of the learning community and can be their whole selves, bringing all that they are.

We've always been committed to making sure every child feels welcome. Although we've both taught several different grades between kindergarten and fifth, we both have a commitment to all that we learned about early childhood education and how important some of those principles are beyond the age of eight. We share beliefs rooted in the work of Reggio Emilia and the idea of the third teacher being the environment. We believe strongly in the words of Loris Malaguzzi, the early childhood educator and founder of the Reggio Emilia Approach, which aims to enable children to construct their understanding of the world through more than just words, using what is available in their environment to facilitate expression. He said, "There are three teachers of children: adults, other children, and their physical environment." We know the power the environment has on learning.

When we originally began to think about creating a comfortable classroom, we thought about soft couches, beanbag chairs, and seats where children could move and bounce if needed. But we've realized that we want so much more for our children than physical comfort: We want our students to feel comfortable emotionally, intellectually, and physically. We want to create a space where each child is comfortable being who they are and learning and growing in a community. We want to create a space where every child has agency as a learner and as a human being.

We want spaces that are flexible and that students can reconfigure and use as needed.

Our Journey with Classroom Design

To teach in a manner that respects and cares for the souls of our students is essential if we are to provide the necessary conditions where learning can most deeply and intimately begin.

— bell hooks, *Teaching to Transgress: Education as the Practice of Freedom* (1994)

This bell hooks quote brings us back to what we know is essential in our teaching: caring for the souls of our students. Lynsey can vividly remember dreaming of what her classroom was going to look like as she neared the end of her student teaching. She would frequently browse the local teacher supply stores and make lists of what she wanted to buy. She picked out "cute" borders and banners to hang. She bought decorations that matched and reflected the colors she liked. When she got her first peek into her new classroom, she thought of all the ways she would make the space hers. Her classroom.

But as we grew and learned together about the necessary conditions for learning, we soon realized the classroom belongs to the children. We needed to cultivate a learning environment that included spaces where student agency was encouraged, freedom wasn't just an invitation but rather a lived experience, identity building was ongoing, and the community was the center. So, we worked to create classroom environments that did not belong to us but rather belonged to the community.

In any classroom environment, we are working toward creating a space where the students are reflected and purposefully considered in the design. We know the multiple ways students learn and think, whether in community or alone. As spaces are created and learning is displayed and curated, the students need to be at the center of this work.

Our thinking about our classroom environment has always been important. But we really started to understand the science behind what we committed to through reading about and studying classroom design. It was more than a decade ago that we started making the shift from creating cozy, comfortable spaces to understanding the science of room design to creating spaces that empower our community of learners.

The Third Teacher: 79 Ways You Can Use Design to Transform Teaching and Learning (2010) was our first step into this work, and that book led us to several experts in the field of school design. The book pushed us to consider how traditional ways of thinking about classroom design did not meet the needs of all learners. It is a book we revisit often. *The Language of School Design* (2009) was also instrumental in helping us understand that there is a science behind innovative school design and the ways design deeply impacts student learning. *The Language of School Design* gave us a way to name some of the things we had in place in our own classroom designs and to reflect and revise in order to better align our designs to our pedagogy. We thought more about all the learning modalities and learning experiences we wanted our learners to have in our classrooms. These books, as well as speakers we heard at conferences, helped us understand classroom design in new ways and helped us better understand our own design process. This work over several years helped us to envision what was possible for our young learners.

The Spaces We Create

Classroom as Coffee Shop

Coffee shops are lively yet quiet enough to write in. They are great places to be alone with a book or to socialize or to work on a project with colleagues. They are great spots for meetings. We loved the idea of people coming together to talk and enjoy each other's company. We had always loved the idea of a "coffee shop feel" in a classroom, but our reading helped us understand why a coffee shop environment matched our vision as a great space for learning. We both visit coffee shops regularly and love the options they provide.

One of our main takeaways from our learning about classroom design was the idea

We want spaces where students can learn on their own.

that we needed different kinds of spaces for different types of learning. Classrooms and schools should offer space to learn in small groups, space for independent learning, space to learn from others, and space to come together as a community. When we think of these ideas, we think of our favorite coffee shops and independent bookstores, which often have quiet corners to sit alone, places where groups can gather, and flexible spaces for large-group events. We noticed this often happens by moving furniture out of the way to create an open area for a speaker and a group.

David Thornburg's learning spaces, especially his metaphors of a campfire, watering hole, and cave, helped us think deeply about the kinds of spaces learners need. His work helped us to understand how authentic learning has worked for centuries and that learners sometimes gather to learn from an expert, sometimes gather to learn with a small group, and sometimes learn from being alone with time to think and reflect. His metaphors are a powerful tool for thinking about classroom design.

Learning the science behind innovative school and classroom design helped us see what our classrooms were and what they were not. Looking at our spaces with fresh eyes allowed us to explore new possibilities and to be honest about the students whose needs were not being met in more traditional classroom settings. We know that we want all these opportunities for our students and that not every student will need the same thing at the same time. If we truly want students to own their own learning, this space must be inclusive of learners' needs and be flexible on a daily (or hourly) basis.

We want spaces where students can think and collaborate with peers.

Flexible Seating

The work we've done over the years around school design has also led us to uncover data behind the things we were noticing in the classroom. Flexible seating had been something we'd been thinking about long before we learned about school design. We always wanted options for student seating. Early in her career, Franki had a bathtub in her classroom, where her first graders could read during reading time. As time went on, she brought in a sofa and beanbag chairs. These were all popular seats. Over the years, we added stools, chairs with some bounce, and cushions to the options our students had throughout the day. We slowly moved away from assigned seats but still had enough "traditional" seats for every child in the classroom. But as we watched our students, the traditional seats were not being used as often as the others, and there was almost never a time when students used more than half of the traditional seats. So, we no longer worried about having enough traditional seats and had other seating options.

We saw firsthand that when students could make choices and decisions about their learning on a day-to-day basis, they learned more. But it was helpful for us to see that existing research found the same thing. The Hechinger Report's "The Students Are Rethinking Classroom Design to Encourage Collaboration, Creativity" by Brenda Lasevoli (2019) shares some insights on school design from several recent studies. We were especially interested to read that "Barrett's study of 153 U.K. classrooms in 27 schools found that adjusting classroom characteristics — light and temperature, the amount of flexibility and student choice — boosted academic performance in reading, writing and math by 16 percent over the course of a year. A quarter of that improvement was attributed to letting students decide when to get up and where to sit."

Classroom Design and Learning Pedagogy

Our schools are designed to prepare children to take their assumed place in the social order rather than to question and challenge that order.

— Carla Shalaby

It is only recently that we've started to realize the ways in which our pedagogy and our room and classroom library design have evolved together and how pedagogy and classroom design cannot be separate.

Our learning about classroom design did not come only from the experts who design schools for a living. Much of our learning came from education scholars and experts whose work transformed our teaching. From bell hooks, we learned about beloved community and our role in creating environments where all students in our care feel safe, loved, and valued.

> "It is only recently that we've started to realize the ways in which our pedagogy and our room and classroom library design have evolved together, and how pedagogy and classroom design cannot be separate."

From Paolo Freire in *We Make the Road by Walking*, we learned about our role. We read and reread his quote, "The teacher is of course an artist, but being an artist does not mean that he or she can make the profile, can shape the students. What the educator does in teaching is to make it possible for the students to become themselves." Freire's words help us to be accountable for the ways our classroom design functions for every child in our care.

From Dr. Gloria Ladson-Billings we learned the power of a community of learners. In her book, *Culturally Relevant Pedagogy: Asking a Different Question* (2021), she notes, "The culturally relevant teachers encouraged a community of learners rather than competitive, individual achievement. By demanding a higher level of academic success for the entire class, individual success did not suffer."

From Peter Johnston in *Choice Words: How Language Affects Children's Learning* (2004), we learned about the power of our words as well as the importance of children talking to and with each other. It was Johnston who helped us truly understand the ideas of identity and agency as these relate to young children's learning.

From Debbie Miller's *Teaching with Intention: Defining Beliefs, Aligning Practices, Taking Action, K–5* (2008), we began to more deeply understand the ways in which our environment must match our beliefs about teaching and learning. Miller also introduced us to the ways in which community and learning intersect, and we began to understand that our classrooms are not merely a community but an intellectual learning community. Miller also taught us the power of putting children's thinking on display.

From Dr. Gholdy Muhammad, we learned how identity, skills, intellect, and criticality work together. Dr. Muhammad asks us to think about these four questions as they relate to instruction:

- **Identity:** How will my instruction help students learn something about themselves and/or about others?
- **Skills:** How will my instruction build students' skills for the content area?
- **Intellect:** How will my instruction build students' knowledge and mental powers?
- **Criticality:** How will my instruction engage students' thinking about power and equity and the disruption of oppression?

After learning from Dr. Muhammad, we began to ask ourselves these same questions but as they related to our classroom and classroom library design:

- **Identity:** How will the classroom and classroom library design help students learn something about themselves and/or about others?
- **Skills:** How will the classroom environment and design build students' skills for the content area?
- **Intellect:** How will the classroom and classroom library design build students' knowledge and mental powers?
- **Criticality:** How will the classroom and classroom library design engage students' thinking about power and equity and the disruption of oppression?

Our classroom environments evolved the most after reading Carla Shalaby's book, *Troublemakers: Lessons in Freedom from Young Children at School* (2017), another book that was not about school design. However, it was transformative for both of us and helped us see how much of traditional classroom design was more about managing and controlling children rather than supporting them as whole human beings. It was *Troublemakers*

TIP: More About Mindset Than Resources

We've learned that classroom design for student agency is more about a mindset than about the resources we have. Learning about classroom design and our own beliefs regarding the way a classroom should run has helped us to see the subtle ways classroom design is sometimes used to control or manage students. We push back on that with a focus on student agency as the goal of classroom design. As much as we love a room with new innovative furniture, lots of space, and funds for redesigning that space, the reality is that most of the rooms we've taught in have been filled with traditional furniture and teaching tools. Throughout this book, you'll see the ways teachers have reimagined the space to create more opportunities for students. The spaces are intentional. Some of the furniture is purchased while some is repurposed. The key is the way the teachers have thought about the space, the mindset to design a room in a way that pushes back on the furniture we are often given and the ways it is traditionally used.

We want spaces that invite various group sizes to gather for learning.

that forced us to look more closely at the teacher-student power structure in place and to really analyze the true choices our students had (or didn't have) every day as learners. We realized, after reading *Troublemakers*, watching and listening to our students, and hearing ourselves, that the spaces we create and the ways we use them deliver big messages about power and control. If we want our students to truly have agency, to be free, to learn, and to be their whole selves, our classroom design must be about those things rather than management and control.

The less we control and manage and the more we commit to freedom, the more our students learn. So, here we are, realizing after decades of teaching that our classroom design is not about creating a cute space but is instead about creating a space in which every child in our care can be free to grow and learn.

Agency, Freedom, Identity Building, Community

The environment should act as an aquarium which reflects the ideas, ethics, attitudes, and the culture of the people who live in it. This is what we are working towards.

— Loris Malaguzzi

When we think about student agency, much of our understanding came from reading *Choice Words: How Our Language Affects Children's Learning* (2003) by Peter Johnston, who says, "Children should leave school with a sense that if they act, and act strategically, they can accomplish their goals. I call this a sense of agency."

Because we are committed to student agency, we are also committed to choice. "Choice is central to agency," Johnston notes. This means that we believe it is important for students to regularly have choice in where they sit, who they sit with, and the materials they use. This does not mean that they have choice 100 percent of the time, but classrooms should be designed with student choice and decision making as the driving forces.

We want to create a space in which every child can be successful and can be a contributing member of our intellectual community. We also want students to build identities as learners, and all of this is dependent on choice. This is how we help every child bring their whole self to the classroom.

Agency and Identity

Facilitating agency and identity building in the classroom results in students who:

- are confident in their own thinking and their ability to learn;
- are coming to know their needs and preferences as learners;
- feel empowered to make choices that match the purpose of their learning;
- feel excited to change and grow as thinkers and learners;
- are respectful and open to the thinking of others that may differ from their own;
- understand that their thinking is valued and an important part of the entire community's learning;
- understand the power of building on the thinking of others;
- value collective thinking and intellectual discourse;
- understand that learning is a process and mistakes and changes are part of that process;
- know their needs as learners and as humans; and
- begin to see how their strengths and traits contribute to their learning.

We want to see students jump up and grab a book from our classroom library at the right moment when they know they need something to support their reading and writing; we want students to feel free to create new book bins with collections of books they want to explore or want others in the community to explore; we want students to walk to the cabinet to grab the felt-tip pens they need for the work they are doing; and we want students to be confident in letting us know when something in the classroom is not working, when something is not meeting their needs as a learner.

If we truly want a space where student agency is valued, it is critical that this space is co-created as a community. The teacher and students should work together to use the room to meet the needs of the community. If the community decides that certain spaces work best for quietly reading and others work best for small-group reading, they have the onus to live in the space that way.

If we want student agency, the space we design must provide choice in all things. One of our favorite quotes about agency is from early childhood educators Shannon Mereinstein and Bar Rucci, who said, "Children know when they are in a space of agency because they feel supported in their choices and safe to be who they are."

We want spaces that invite a variety of group configurations for learning depending on student needs.

Building an Intellectual Community

For students to have agency as learners, they must be part of an intellectual community. Building an intellectual community is a bit different than building just any community for other purposes. An intellectual community, to us, means a community that comes together for learning and for growing. The community is made up of individuals who bring their whole selves to the learning. And together, everyone learns more because it is the collective — the coming together of individual voices — that is the power behind the intellectual community.

We know much of the community is built on relationships, and our classrooms are designed to support the building of relationships between teacher and student and between individual students. It is also built to give students time to build a positive relationship with learning. For this to happen, we must genuinely see our students as equal partners. As Dr. Mariana Souto-Manning says, "Culturally relevant teachers regard their students capably — as persons from whom they should learn."

An intellectual community means that every member is valued for who they are. Classroom design is the first and most effective way to level the playing field in the classroom because every voice is equal when the power structure is shifted. An intellectual community requires spaces and tools for practicing intellectual thinking. That may happen in a variety of spaces and with different members of the community. It is in these spaces that our children learn they are trusted and valued members of the learning community.

When students are empowered to make choices, they come to know and trust themselves as learners and can confidently build on the thinking of others. In this way, it is the collective thinking that is transformational.

We want a variety of seating options for children to choose from.

Continuing Our Journey

When we talk about the classroom as the third teacher, we understand that every decision we make about room design can either be a support or an obstacle to student learning. If we choose to have individual student desks spread across the room, we limit the amount of authentic talk that can happen between students. If we decide not to have a teacher desk, we are more likely to engage directly with students for more minutes of each day. When we place books on a shelf that is inaccessible to children because we don't want students to tear them, we send the message that we control the learning tools. When we begin to think of every design decision as one of utmost importance and then make changes accordingly, we can disrupt the power structure apparent in traditional classrooms.

When we think of designing classrooms for student agency, we want to provide all children with the types of spaces and tools they need to grow and learn. We want them to have confidence to make choices and to come to know themselves and their needs as learners. We want a space that gives every child the message, "we trust you." We want them to know they are a valued part of an intellectual community, not only because it recognizes them as human beings with agency but also because it leads to improved learning outcomes. This book is a compilation of what has worked well for us (and for a few of our colleagues), and we hope it helps you to re-envision not only what your classroom can be but also the why of your decisions as you think about the impact your classroom and classroom library design have on each child in your care.

We want spaces where students can take the lead in facilitating learning.

Part 1

Classroom Design

Designing for Student Agency

Students can make choices about the best places to do their learning at any given time.

Supporting student agency is at the heart of all we do, and our classroom design has evolved the more we understand the idea of agency. We have both been thinking about and learning about agency for decades. Although self-efficacy and growth mindset are often talked about when thinking about learner agency, agency is about more than a learner's beliefs or confidence. Certainly, a belief that you can grow and learn is a piece of student agency, but it is certainly not the whole picture.

There is so much to student agency that we like to pull from a variety of resources when we define it for ourselves. Of course, we have learned so much from Peter Johnston (*Choice Words*), but we've learned from so many others as well. Following are some quotes with key points about student agency that help us create a vision for the classrooms we want to create.

- "Student agency includes a capacity for self-efficacy but also requires the intentional forethought to set a course of action and adjust it as needed to fulfill one's goal."
  – *Teaching Kids to Thrive*, Corwin, 2017, p. 69
- "Agency is inherent in students' ability to regulate, control, and monitor their own learning. A learners' effectiveness in regulating their cognitive, affective, and behavioral

processes as they interact within the learning environment is critical to their academic success."
— Article by Jillianne Code, "Agency for Learning: Intention, Motivation, Self-Efficacy and Self-Regulation," 2020, *Frontiers in Education* (www.frontiersin.org/articles/10.3389/feduc.2020.00019/full)

- "Agency is the capability of individuals to make choices and to act on those choices in ways that make a difference in their lives."
  — Code, "Agency for Learning"
- "Agency is in operation only when individuals self-reflect and identify external influences that are most nurturing to the self."
  — Code, "Agency for Learning"
- "Learner agency is about having the power, combined with choices, to take meaningful action and see the results of your decisions."
  — *What Is Learner Agency*, Inspiring Inquiry (www.inspiringinquiry.com/the-learner/learner-agency)

When we consider all that we understand about learner agency, we can design rooms that give children the tools and time to be empowered as learners. We know that classroom design is the first step to inclusive practices. As Tricia Ebarvia states in the blog, *How Inclusive Is Your Literacy Classroom Really*?: "Inclusive practices are those that guarantee the perspectives and contributions of all people — especially of diverse backgrounds who have been traditionally marginalized such as LGBTQ+ individuals, people with disabilities, and people of color — are given equal recognition, attention, and care in all learning environments."

So, we constantly ask ourselves these questions as we design and build community in our classrooms:

- Do students have access to all learning tools?
- Is there anything that is "off

When we are committed to student agency, the notes we take about student learning are not a secret. We share these with students at conferences, when goal-setting together, or to let children know why we are moving in a certain way with mini-lesson work.

Students know that their thinking is valued and that their learning might help others, just as others' learning helps them.

limits" to students? If so, why is that, and how can I change that?
- Can students access anything they need without asking for teacher permission? If not, why is that, and how can I change it?
- Do students have choice in the ways they approach learning activities and projects and choice in the tools they use to accomplish goals? If not, why is that, and how can I change it?
- Are students involved in their own goal setting and in making plans to achieve goals? If not, why is that, and how can I change it?
- Are students given opportunities to see what is possible as learners? How do we accomplish this?
- Do students have choice in where they sit, who they work with, and how they approach tasks? Where, when, and why do I limit choices?
- Am I open to students approaching tasks in a different way than the ways I imagined they might?
- How is each space inclusive of students' identities?
- How is the wall space positioned as a learning tool?
- What is visually privileged on the walls, in book displays, and throughout the classroom?
- Whose work/thinking takes up space on the walls of the classroom?
- How do I make student learning visible and make sure that reflection of learning is valued by students?

When we think about room design for student agency, we have many nonnegotiables. These include:

- choice and options in seating;
- choice in tools and the ability to use tools in new ways;
- choice in how learners approach tasks;
- opportunities to learn from and with each other;
- opportunities to create new spaces and groupings;
- access to all tools at all times; and
- spaces to make student thinking and learning visible.

The most important component of room design is that we trust our students to use this space and these learning tools in ways that work for them.

Students can decide on a space that works for them when they need to talk with peers to move forward as learners. This is their decision.

Students always have access to pencils and paper as well as to digital tools.

The document camera is available to students as needed. This student is asking for writing feedback from the whole class.

All the elements in the room are available to students. Nothing is off-limits for children to use, and choosing which tools to use and how to use them is an indication of student agency.

We purposely use notebooks with blank pages so students can plan and design annotations on their own. We do not limit choices with lines or graphic organizers. Choosing the ways to organize thinking, as well as the writing tools that will best allow them to do that, is critical.

We are purposeful in setting up our whole-class space so the teacher can facilitate from various places rather than teaching from the front of the room.

Students have access to individual and community supplies. And all tools are easily accessible so teachers and students can use the tools stored throughout the room when they need them.

We choose seating options that make it easy for young children to move as needed.

A student is looking at a calendar of book sharing that is always available.

* Various Spaces for Different Configurations for Learning

We have come to realize that classroom design isn't something you do at the start of the year, and then it's done. Of course, you will always have parts and pieces that remain in place, but naturally, as students begin to learn how they want to use the space for learning, the room starts to shift and change. It comes alive and grows alongside the learners who inhabit it. For this reason, we work to think about our initial classroom design as configurations for learning.

> "Over the years, we have learned that we have to prioritize spaces in order to create the spaces we need."

To stay committed to the thought of an initial classroom design, we reflect by asking ourselves questions like these:

1. How might the learning look in this space?
2. Do we have spaces for quiet learning?
3. Do we have spaces where our students can engage in vibrant discourse?
4. Are spaces inclusive of all physical abilities, learning needs, sensory needs, and emotional needs?
5. Are there large spaces where learners can spread out and gather around a variety of tools?
6. Are there spaces where solitude can be created?
7. Are there spaces where a few students can gather?

Just like many of you have experienced over a summer, classrooms get their necessary deep cleaning, and furniture is pushed to the center of the room or off to the side. This is a practice that happens every year for us. Many of those years, we worked quickly in August to put the room back together just as it had been the year prior, but throughout this journey, we realized we were missing a great opportunity to reflect and to be intentional about creating the configurations for learning that would support student agency.

Recently, Lynsey took pictures of her process of configuring the classroom after a summer deep clean. Over the years, we have learned that we have to prioritize spaces in order to create the spaces we need. For a while, our default was to think about individual student seating first, since that took up so much space. But then there was often little space left over once that was in place. Instead, we now think about what is most important to the learning community and begin with those important spaces. And within those priorities, we think about the flexibility of seating for each space.

One configuration for learning that we prioritize is the meeting space. The meeting space is where the whole class can come together in a close space to continuously foster the growth of the intellectual learning community. Typically, this is the first space created, and then from there, the rest of the room is designed by the types of learning and use of the classroom we invite students to create for themselves. There are many ways to design a classroom at the beginning of the year to send students messages about the year ahead. No matter how we set the classroom up, the goals are the same.

Lynsey knew she needed:

1. *A whole-group meeting space*
2. *Partner spaces*
3. *Small group spaces*
4. *Large empty floor spaces*
5. *Standing working spaces*
6. *Floor-sitting working spaces*
7. *Classroom library*
8. *Student access to learning tools*

Lynsey also knew she wanted all students to be able to move freely about the room from space to space. Room flow was important as she thought about where quiet spaces may be or where students who needed to work and talk together could go. Lynsey also knew she could use furniture to make defined spaces that could move if needed.

This is the result of Lynsey's room design.

Another year, in the same room, Lynsey started the year off a little differently.

Whole-Group Spaces

The first day of school in Lynsey's third-grade classroom, the class gathers in the whole-group meeting space to read a book together. This whole-group meeting space is an important part of creating agentive learners: this is where readers and writers meet to build upon each other's ideas, ask questions, think out loud alongside their peers, and cultivate a safe learning space in which to take risks.

On this day, the new group of third graders discussed what their perfect day would be. (They were reading *A Perfect Day* by Lane Smith.) Unprompted, a student named Garrett spoke up and said, "What is everyone's favorite day?" Lynsey knew she had to pause and see what these new students would do. It only took a second for the classroom to buzz with excitement and sharing around Garrett's question.

Lynsey stood back and watched as her new class began to navigate the meeting space. It was around 10:30 a.m. on the first day of school, and Lynsey was able to watch and take notes on the early dynamics of the meeting space.

The Whole-Class Meeting Area

One of the things we want students to know and feel about the whole-group meeting space is that they have power in this space. This space is for them to grow as readers and writers, and what happens is this space is directly related to what they need as growing readers and writers. We accomplish this by keeping the meeting space a regular part of our daily routine. We meet there anytime the whole group needs to learn and think together.

Another thing we want our students to know and feel about the meeting space is that everyone must have a voice. The space is designed so that students can easily turn and see the speaker. It's also designed in such a way that the speaker can be in front, in back, in the middle, off to the side, or anywhere around the space. There is no "front of the room" in this space. We work to cultivate an environment where the students want to hear from all their peers and work to listen to the words they are communicating and sharing with the group.

Lastly, it is important for our students to know and feel that when we come together in this space, we are an intellectual community of learners. As such, we take care of each other's intellectual, emotional, and physical safety in this space.

Listening to Students about the Space

It was mid-fall in Lynsey's room when students spoke up about the physical meeting area. It was Anya who first said, "Mrs. Burkins, it's hard to see everyone, and it feels weird when we are trying to talk to some people high up at the table when we are on the floor."

Brianna added, "What do you think we should do about it?" Lynsey walked to the whiteboard and wrote down Anya's words and Brianna's words. She knew it was important for

Whole-class space in a first-grade classroom.

Lynsey's third-grade class shares a book together in the whole-group space.

Our whole-group area has plenty of space for children to spread out with their learning tools. We also want them to make sure they have sufficient space to turn and talk with a partner.

her to listen carefully as the class voiced their concerns and showed willingness to problem-solve. As students began talking, Lynsey wrote down their suggestions and comments. It was Enzo who finally said, "Let's move things around to see what will work for everyone!"

The class got busy talking about plans — what should move and what should stay. Lynsey asked follow-up questions and nudged students to go deeper in their responses toward one another. The students decided on a configuration that made for more students sitting on the carpet, and they moved one of the tables to the hallway space, opening the carpet space by placing a rolling cart nearby so that students could have a place to display their work on the document camera that wouldn't interrupt other students sitting on the carpet.

Ann Marie Corgill's whole-group spaces are always designed to support the intellectual community. Having some type of border around the perimeter of the whole-class space gives options for seating.

Opportunities for Circle

Indigenous peoples around the world have clearly used circles to attend to the community's work.

— Living Justice Press

In 2017, Lynsey came across a blog post, *The Indigenous Origins of Circles and How Non-Natives Learned about Them*, reprinted from Living Justice Press. That led her to start researching talking circles as a restorative practice in the classroom. Later, in 2019, she attended the National Education Association's conference on Race and Social Justice. As she listened, captivated by a session about the use of restorative circles in schools, she knew she had to keep learning about the power of gathering in a circle. It was clear that the practice of a talking circle was essential when healing and restoring a community, but she also wondered about the potential it had when it came to learning from one another and building a community of readers and writers.

Questions we ask ourselves as literacy teachers about our learning spaces and practices include:

1. When do learners have opportunities to talk to each other?
2. When do learners have opportunities to engage in discourse with more than another person?
3. When do learners have time to listen to one another?
4. When do learners gather in a space to practice speaking and listening?
5. Does the space allow for speaking, listening, and learning/unlearning from one another?

Whole-group spaces have similar features in that they offer space for the whole group to gather for a variety of purposes. Community learning is visible in the space, and there is a clear border that often invites another layer of seating.

Listening to 5th Graders about Whole-Class Space

Franki began creating space for a circle during her years teaching fifth grade. She noticed that colleague Max Brand's students were always in a circle when she visited his classroom, and she asked him the reason behind it. He said it was the best way to learn to have conversations in which everyone had a voice, where students could learn to have genuine conversations without hand raising, and where everyone was able to see and hear everyone else. It created an equal space for everyone.

For years after, Franki's students sat in a circle during read-aloud. To listen to her students, she would take a seat in the circle between two students. She sat beside different people every day, so she was able to listen closely to conversations during "Turn and Talk."

One year, in the winter, she noticed several students began complaining about sitting on the floor. She had noticed that the circle was getting more crowded as the children

When we think of attending to the community's work, we imagine the work to look like this.

were growing (as they do a LOT in fifth grade). Franki talked to them about her purpose for the circle, and some shared again about how uncomfortable the floor was getting as they grew. The class came up with a solution and created a two-layer circle where students who were most comfortable on the floor could sit on the floor, and those who preferred a bench or stool could do that. She added a bench to the perimeter of the space and added stackable stools of varying heights.

In essence, they created a double circle, and thus all needs were met. Students could still see and hear everyone, and no single person was centered. Plus, everyone was comfortable and more engaged in the learning. We've held onto this idea of a layer of seats around the perimeter of the whole-group space as we remain committed to options for our students in all areas of the classroom. Listening to our students has led us to create flexible seating options within the whole class space.

Opportunities for Turn and Talk Within Whole-Group Space

One of our goals for the whole-group meeting space is to teach our learners that they are welcome to have a voice in the group setting of their peers and that they are welcome to speak just one on one. There are many times during the whole-group instructional times where the Turn and Talk opportunity is agentive for our students. Students learn that they can suggest points during instruction where they feel like a Turn and Talk would be helpful to their learning.

Our learners learn that they can practice what they want to say with a partner before offering their ideas to the larger

The whole-group meeting space must have room enough for readers and writers to converse together and converse in pairs. We call this opportunity to stop and think with another person the "Turn and Talk."

In the whole-class space, students are also engaged in a text that is projected on the board. The space is designed for study and conversation, for independent thought within community conversation.

group. Students also learn that a Thinking Partner can help them discover, learn, and unlearn information as they are on their learning journey.

Some students need to talk out their thinking to make sense of things; others need to jot ideas down before they are ready to talk. We want all students to have the space they need to do the thinking, sharing, and building on others' thinking— it is important that we ensure all students have the time and tools they need to be able to participate in the co-constructed thinking.

Our whole-group space needs to not only be large enough for our students to gather, but it also needs to provide enough space for learners to turn to a partner and to work with a notebook, a laptop, or other tools in order to make sense of their thinking.

Opportunities for Various Things to Be Centered

Usually in whole-class teaching spaces, the teacher is centered. Students are facing the "front" and the teacher facilitates learning from the front of the room. While this is an option for some times during whole-class instruction, we must ask ourselves, "If we are committed to student agency, what should be centered during whole-class instruction?"

Instead of the teacher, we want the community to be centered, so Lynsey has been creating spaces where she can facilitate from several places in the room. In this way, she centers the text and the community conversation rather than herself. She often walks around the perimeter of the space, takes a seat with the class, or stands at the back of the room during whole-class instruction.

Whole-Group Space: What's Important?

This higher level of seating on the perimeter of the whole-group space has become important, as it gives choices and options for students within this space.

We design our whole-class space with all these things in mind. First and foremost, we want a space where everyone can come together as learners to think and grow together. We know that at times, we'll want to sit in a larger circle, so we'll need to have space for that. We also know that we'll want various things to be centered, so we'll set up for that, too. We know our learners will come to this space with thinking tools, so they need space to spread out just a bit. And we know that we'll want space for readers and writers to Turn and Talk and to collaborate within our whole-class time. Thus, the whole-class space is designed with all of this in mind. The space must accommodate the whole class in various configurations.

*Independent Learning Spaces

Many different spaces in the room can serve many purposes. Students can use a space to gather and collaborate or they can create spaces within a larger space for independent reading and writing.

"Mrs. Burkins!" Enzo yelled across the room. "I just need a space to get away from it all and write my story."

Lynsey chuckled to herself at Enzo's choice of words, but she was also encouraged as she watched him create the perfect space to "get away from it all."

Independent working spaces are vital if we want to foster agentive free learners. How many times as adults do we feel the need to be alone in order to work and think? The option of having the autonomy to create a space where alone time can occur has the power to help students produce the work required of them.

Sometimes in classrooms, only individual workspaces or only small-group workspaces are available. Early on in her teaching, Lynsey was excited to have tables at which students could sit together, and her classroom was filled with rectangular tables that sat four students. She loved the shift from individual desks to tables, but she soon realized no single grouping worked in all situations.

When we create alone spaces throughout the classroom, this sends the message that independent learning is valued as one way, but not the only way, that we learn. When we provide tools for students to create their own independent spaces, we build agency as they get the message that they have control over their learning and that we trust they know their learning needs at any given time.

When we have tools needed—portable stools, cushions, clipboards, and laptops—our learners begin to create the spaces they need for the learning they are doing.

We know that learners need different types of spaces to do different types of learning. They also need different tools based on the learning they are doing. As we set up our classrooms, we must set up spaces that invite students to be independent in their learning and to envision what type of work they may do in a space.

Small-Group Spaces

Sometimes readers and writers like to work independently while sitting with a small group. They know that much of their writing work is independent but that there may be times throughout the workshop when they need a thinking partner. Several spaces in the classroom allow for this type of small group.

Small groups are at the heart of our classrooms. Gathering with friends to think through an issue in a book or to solve a problem from recess helps build intellectual thinking. Our students gather throughout the day for various reasons. We want them to know when it makes sense to work with a group and when it makes sense to work independently. Sometimes groups gather around a common book; other times they are thinking about something together. Sometimes groups need areas where they can explore something without worrying about the noise they are making. Other times, small groups want a quieter space. Our classrooms are designed to allow for all of these configurations, and our students are masterful at rearranging furniture to meet their needs at any given time. When we trust students to determine where and with whom they will work, they become more independent learners.

Depending on the time of the day and the work at hand, students choose seating and groupings that work for them in the moment. Being able to choose a spot for a particular purpose is important, and children find various spots for various purposes throughout the day.

We know that sometimes small groups of readers and writers want to meet at a table. We have options for that throughout the room.

Some spaces are better for groups who have books, tools, and writing to spread out.

Ann Marie Corgill sets up several spaces that invite partner and small-group work.

There are always options for pushing two areas together to create an area that can accommodate a larger group.

Spaces for Partners

Partners often create their own space to read together.

We recently realized how often our students choose to work with just one other person throughout the day. When students have choices, we notice patterns, and one pattern we notice with preschool through sixth grade is that working with one trusted peer is a choice our learners often make. The partner groups shift as children choose to work with different people throughout the day, but partnering seems to be a preference year after year. When we look across the room, we always notice various configurations, but over the years we've come to realize that partner work is valued and is the configuration we see most often around the classroom.

Because we have routines such as Turn and Talk and Thinking Partners in place where we invite readers and writers to talk and think with another person during our whole class instruction, our readers and writers are used to conferring with one other peer. They do this as they think through the theme of a book or get feedback on a recent piece of writing. We think these routines have helped our learners see the power of thinking with another person, and in turn, they choose partner work more often.

We don't tend to create many spaces that are set up for partners, as we've discovered many of the partner spaces our students find are not necessarily set up for two people. Just the same, many spaces simply work well for that. We have noticed, however, that often when students choose to work with one other person, they prefer to sit side by side. This discovery has helped us create spaces that invite side-by-side partner work.

Spaces like this one can be used for independent reading, and they also provide the perfect spot for exploring a book together.

Partners often create their own space to write together.

These students have created their own space and gathered the tools needed to work on a piece of writing together.

A space like this one in Lauren Scott's kindergarten classroom invites children to work independently or to move over one of the chairs and work side by side.

A bench that stores student book bins is also a favorite spot for partner work.

Once we realized side-by-side partner work was important for our learners, we created more spaces that invited this as an option.

Creating Flexible Spaces and Flexible Seating

We often design the whole-class space with benches or tables around the perimeter, knowing that those pieces of furniture will be used in different ways at other times during the day.

In our classrooms, we want both flexible space and flexible seating. By flexible space, we mean we want space that can be used in multiple ways — space that invites reconfiguration for different purposes. In terms of flexible seating, we want our students to have choices, a variety of options for learning spaces. Some tasks require a table space while for other learning, the floor may be the best spot. As we support student agency, we want them to be intentional about their use of space, and we know children will choose a variety of seats throughout the day.

Note: When we say "seats," we are referring to "locations," as some students often choose standing up. We've incorporated standing desks/taller tables as an option.

We create spaces that are flexible in a variety of ways. Tables on wheels, various portable seating options, and furniture that can be used as both a seat and a table help with this.

The whole-group meeting area is one of our most flexible spaces. It can be used for whole-group instruction, but it can also be used in multiple ways at other times during the day. Students can gather in groups, spread out with tools on the floor, or push the benches together to make a small-group space. This is one of the most used spaces in the classroom because of the flexibility it offers.

Multiple Seating Options for Flexible Seating

We like to have many options for children when we think about seating. These trays allow children to choose the floor as a learning space. This is a great option for learning from informational videos such as Friends with Fins *by Jaclyn Friendlander (2014).*

We moved away from assigned seats years ago. We were both in classrooms with individual traditional seating, and every child was assigned a desk. Neither of us have ever been teachers to have desks in rows; we've always been committed to collaborative workspace. So, when desks were what we were given, we put those in clusters and tried various ways to make the seating work.

It didn't take us long to realize that assigned seats were limiting if for no other reason than from a management perspective. If children were working on a project with someone who did not sit near them, they would have to ask to use that person's desk. Students took strong ownership of their spaces, and there were not many community spaces. We wanted our children to be able to move around and have opportunities to work with a variety of peers, but doing so while having assigned seats was clunky at best.

When we moved away from assigned seats, we were able to replace desks with tables. We also started to think about student supplies and moved toward community supplies for things like markers, scissors, and crayons. For individual supplies, students had book bins, drawer space, and/or individual baskets/trays. This created a better feel, as no one felt ownership of a place simply because it was where their supplies were.

Our first step away from assigned, individual seats was a system in which children would have a name tag, and they would choose a seat for the day. They would place their name tag there to indicate it was their place for that day. We quickly let that go, as it really didn't accomplish anything toward student agency because they could not choose space based on purpose.

Once we let go of any type of assigned seating, we worried about having enough traditional seats in the classroom. So, we made sure that if we had 24 students, we had 24 traditional seats (desks or tables);

all the flexible seating would be extra. Over time, we realized the traditional seating was used less and less. So, we started to worry less about having a class set of traditional seats.

> Sidenote: Some years, we kept traditional seats in place because of testing requirements. Again, we learned that our students were much more comfortable taking tests in the spaces they were most comfortable learning in, and that was seldom a traditional school seat.

Now we set up our classroom with the various spaces we know are important for learning, and we know that students will navigate these spaces and begin to learn what works best for them as learners. We focus on the learning and the flexibility, and so we design a space with a variety of seating options for children to use during the day. It took us years to let go of all the traditional habits we had about student seats, but once we watched the ways in which students used the seating options, we grew more confident in letting those habits go.

Freeing Up Space: Teacher's Desk

Years ago, we decided to get rid of our traditional teacher's desk. At first, we chose this because our teacher space was taking up a huge section of the classroom. By getting rid of our teacher desk or area, we freed up space in the classroom to create other areas for the students to use. And as we began to live in the spaces with students without a teacher's desk, we found that students began to see us more as part of their learning community, not as someone they perceived as the owner of knowledge and controller of the space.

We also realized the message that a teacher desk or area had given our students about unequal power. We were taking up a much larger space in the classroom than anyone else. The message that our work was more important than theirs was a message that space gave without us realizing it.

And, just as our students do each day, we started to find the right space for the right purpose. If we wanted to meet with an individual child about his/her reading, we'd use a space set up for two people. If we wanted to pull together a small group, we'd move tables together to accommodate the group. All the spaces we had created for our students worked for us, too, and we began to use the classroom space as would any other member of the community. Our desks had never really worked for either of us, but we couldn't pinpoint why. Once we began to understand spaces for learning and thinking, and once we began to utilize flexible spaces in more effective ways, it became clear.

We still have shelves and cabinets that house things we need for our work (assessment files, emergency sub plans, etc.), but those take up very little space. We've also devised ways to make sure we have teaching tools necessary for small-group instruction, etc. Some years, we added a cart on wheels that housed assessment forms, sticky notes, etc.; other years, we assigned ourselves a drawer or basket along with the drawers that students used for supplies. If we are serious about student agency, we need to be committed to everyone (students and teachers) having equal access to all the same tools. The only exception we make is the necessarily confidential and safety information.

Not only did seating become flexible, but when children had choice over where to sit and work and could move to various areas across the day based on their purpose, the entire room became flexible. Very little was fixed in a way that could not be changed when needed.

The Message of Tables and Bookshelves on Wheels

Books carts allow spaces to be flexible by not having to keep the books in a fixed space. Sometimes, children will suggest moving the book cart to a more convenient space.

Make it new. Look at your learning space with 21st-century eyes: Does it work for what we know about learning today, or just for what we knew about learning in the past?

— The Third Teacher

Does your classroom space work, given what we know about learning today? When we came across this question while reading *The Third Teacher* years ago, it stuck with us. It is one of those fundamental questions that lingers in our heads each day as we work with children. Does this space work for the learning we are doing today?

Over the past decade, we have noticed a pendulum shift and a new awareness toward the power of movement, specifically in the classroom setting. More recently, we have noticed an increase in the number of ideas related to movement breaks being shared among teachers: movement apps, YouTube movement videos, and general discussion about how to get students moving during the school day. But we can't stop thinking: What if the day was built with movement as a naturally embedded component?

Studies on ergonomics have made their way to looking at school settings, and yet, we are still left with this same question: Do our learning spaces work, given what we know about learning today, or do they just work for what we knew about learning in the past?

One year, while we taught at the same school, we both noticed that students seemed to want to create their own spaces for learning, but the furniture wasn't easily moveable. We were excited about finding taller IKEA tables that were lightweight and didn't take up much space. We also found smaller side tables that provided easy portability. Our students were constantly moving them to create the spaces they needed as their needs changed. We later added wheels to the tables, making them even easier to move around.

The benefit of having moveable furniture wasn't just practical (i.e., that students could organize themselves to work in whatever ways worked best for them). Having moveable furniture also sent a powerful agentive message to students.

5 Messages that Movable Furniture and Flexible Seating Send to Our Students

1 Learning Is Active

When students walk into a classroom space and notice that it is flexible, they can imagine themselves actively engaging in the arrangement of pieces with their needs in mind. Meet the Teacher Day happens each year in our school system on the day before school officially begins. Students excitedly roam the halls in anticipation of meeting their new teacher and seeing the classroom in which they will be living for the year. Students come in and immediately start trying things out and playing in and with the space. This kind of play is essential to building a learning community that will use the space in ways that best support their learning.

2 Spaces Can Be Constructed and Deconstructed

Learning spaces that meet the needs of the specific moment are crucial if students are to make sound decisions about their own learning. Readers and writers may require a variety of spaces throughout one workshop session, and giving them the ability to construct those spaces is essential as we teach them to make decisions that support their reading and writing growth. So, if students know it will help them to pull together a quick writing group to share their work and elicit feedback, they can create a space that does that. Early on, we teach our students through their natural play and curiosity with the furniture that spaces in our classrooms can and should be constructed and deconstructed throughout their learning day.

3 Movement Is Part of the Learning

Movement isn't the break that students get during a transition time; Instead, movement is part of the learning. Students should feel free to get up and grab materials, go ask a quick question, find a book they need to help their reading or writing, or move in their chair while they are writing.

4 Learning Spaces Are Dependent on the Learners' Needs

In Lynsey's current classroom, the interactive board is on wheels. It's the first time in eighteen years she has had this; typically, it is housed in the large-group meeting area. With wheels, however, it can be moved to wherever it's needed throughout the day. Initially, students asked if they could move it to create a space to use with a small group and to read a digital text together. Having the interactive board on wheels indicated that movement mattered and was allowed. These students realized their learning space was dependent on what they needed at that time, and that resource placement wasn't permanent.

5 Creative Spaces Are Welcome

Nontraditional working spaces start with creativity. As students build the spaces they need, they are thinking about how they want to feel while engaging in learning. Lynsey asked her students about the space they created in this picture. This is what one of the students in the first image had to say: "We all wanted to sit together, but we wanted to sit in ways that could help us stay working for a long time. We each got seating tools, and put them how we wanted them so we can think together." We work to provide flexible spaces that students can use in a variety of ways. Having easy-to-move furniture and flexible seating allows students to create these spaces as needed.

When Students Create the Spaces They Need

We love when students create the spaces they need. When they can pull over a dry-erase board, move a table and seats they need together for their group size, and gather all the tools they need, students have ownership of their learning.

When we offer a variety of seating options for children and when the seats are easy to move around the room, children feel comfortable creating spaces that meet their needs as learners.

A stack of cushioned seats next to a bookshelf lets children know they can use those seats wherever they think is best.

When students have various seating options, they find and create spaces that work for the purpose they have and, in turn, are far more engaged and agentive learners.

Sometimes, students can benefit most from working with peers. Other times, they know that thinking alone is best for the learning they are doing. When the room is set up to allow children to find and create the spaces they need, this happens naturally, and children use spaces in unique ways.

When we have furniture on wheels, students can easily push them together to accommodate more people or move them to a spot that has the tools and resources they need. This invites them to try new seating options.

If we are committed to flexible seating and students having ownership of creating needed spaces for learning, our furniture choices must be intentional. Having stackable stools and tables that are easy to move around the room gives students permission to try new seating, various group arrangements, etc.

Making the Best Use of Wall Space

Leah's questions were hung on the wall.

Our journey into thinking about wall space as a catalyst for student agency started long before we could name it. Lynsey vividly remembers as a new teacher poring over the pages of Debbie Miller's *Reading with Meaning* (2002) and stopping for long periods of time to study the inside color photographs of her classroom. Lynsey was drawn to Miller's quote, "Creating classroom environments that are literate, organized, purposeful, and accessible nurture literacy and foster independence." Uncertain what that meant for a new teacher, Lynsey studied the pictures and words of Miller's book for evidence of what a literate, organized, purposeful, and accessible classroom environment actually looked like. One major idea she picked up was the placement of student work around the room — Miller placed students' work alongside teacher-created materials, showing a dual ownership of space. This was one of Lynsey's very first memories on her journey toward classroom design for student agency.

Now, as we both have studied and talked — and studied and talked some more — we could begin to name what we had discovered through practice as ways to use wall space as a catalyst for student agency. We worked toward this by starting the school year with the walls blank, using that space for co-constructed thinking and to amplify student thinking.

Starting with Blank Walls or with Very Temporary Wall Design

Samantha Bennett, author of *That Workshop Book* (2007), teaches that the classroom should be filled with what comes out of the mouths and minds of students. The environment should be built around what students are constructing and thinking. The wall space in our classrooms is essential when crafting a learning environment that mirrors our students. This is why we start the school year with the walls blank: we want students' creations and thinking to fill the walls and grow with the class as the year progresses.

Things That Go on the Walls

1. Examples of student learning
2. Student-created anchor charts
3. Student-created organizational items
4. Students' words and meaning-making
5. Students' questions

"Mrs. Burkins!" Leah called from her comfy spot she had created on the floor. "Can I hang these on the wall so we can think about these questions together?"

Lynsey walked over to see what Leah had created. She read the questions Leah wrote on the pages: Who are we? What do we do? What are we meant for? Why do we hurt animals and they don't hurt us? What can we do to help? Lynsey had so many questions for Leah, but instead she said, "Please tell me more." Leah explained how she wanted the class to think about these questions together and asked if she could put them on the wall so the class could keep thinking about them. Of course, they went on the wall. This taught Lynsey that her students knew the wall space was for them and about them. They knew they could use it for thinking together and to share their thoughts publicly with an audience.

Co-constructed Thinking

Dr. Vivian Maria Vasquez, the author of *Negotiating Critical Literacies with Young Children* (2004), pushed our understanding of making learning visible through her work with audit trails in a classroom of preschool age children. Audit trails are ways that students and the teacher make their learning visible together via the walls of the classroom. The walls are living spaces that tell the story of the learning that is happening and ongoing in the classroom. This is an important component to building an intellectual community. Vasquez states, "As we worked through various critical incidents and issues, the children and I made decisions about what to post. The impact an issue had in the social worlds of the children or the kind of contribution to change in our social spaces determined what was posted."

Amplifying Student Thinking

Lynsey's whiteboard is used to capture student thinking and to use that thinking as springboards to learning.

We have found that fixed bulletin boards and chalkboards on the wall are great spaces designated as spots for student thinking. The goal is for students to use these spots for places to go to look for inspiration, to add an idea, or even just to marvel at the work of their peers. Students can decide on their own what goes up and what can come down to make space for more pieces. For classrooms that do not have these as options, we've used chart paper, removable dry erase sheets, and regular sticky notes on the side of a file cabinet.

Closets can also serve as extended wall space, especially because we want learning to be visible for students. Kindergarteners in Jessica Ardela's room documented their thinking about some picture books here.

Our walls start out blank but are ready for student thinking.

Early in the school year, Lynsey's third graders create their own alphabet chart. It is one of the first things that goes up on the blank walls.

We use backs of bookshelves and cabinets as extra wall space for students to share their learning.

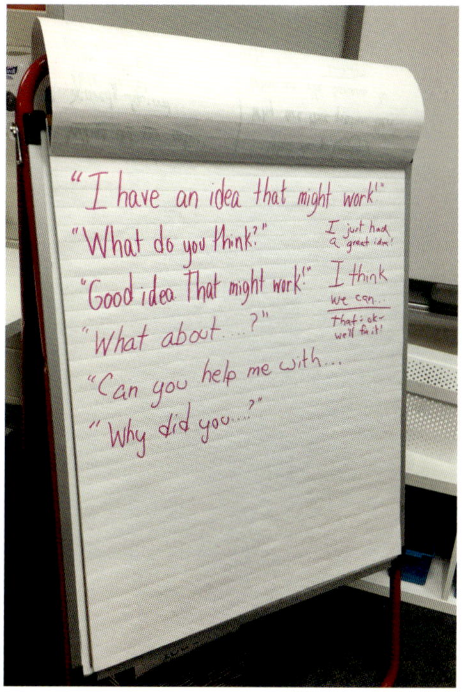

We often chart student language that we hear and then post those more permanently if students use them.

When we don't have large dry-erase boards to use for student thinking, there are other options. In this first-grade classroom, Ana Sibberson created a space for student words using dry-erase removable stickers on a closet door.

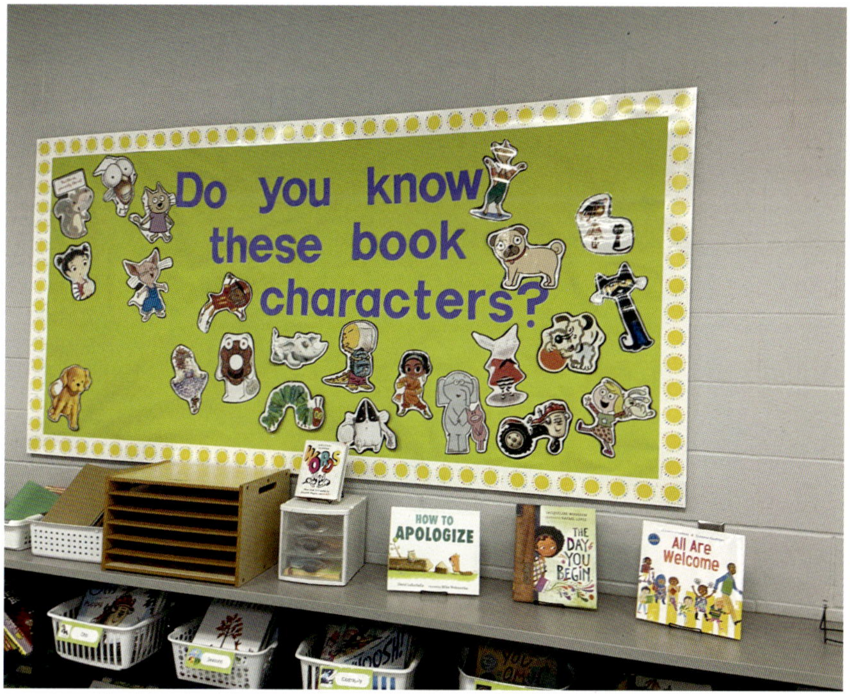

Sometimes instead of blank walls, we use temporary bulletin boards, knowing they will be replaced during the first few days of school with students' thinking. These boards in Ana Sibberson's first-grade room invited conversations between children and their families during open house.

Accessible Tools for Learning

Students have a space for the tools they need as learners. Drawers or baskets house individual students' tools.

Choice is central to student agency and, if we believe in choice, access to tools matters.

We have been thinking about the idea of creating a "YES environment" lately. The National Association for the Education of Young Children (NAEYC) defines a YES environment as "a safe, positive place that encourages personal growth by allowing the freedom of reasonable risk taking" (2019).

When we think about the idea of risk taking in elementary settings as related to a YES environment, we think about the risks children take as learners: risks to try things and to see what works for them. Risk-taking is key to knowing yourself as a learner and to student agency. In the classroom, some of that risk-taking is connected to choosing tools that match learning and purpose.

We have been reflective regarding our own reasons for saying no to certain things. We realized that we used to say no based on what our plans were for the lesson. When we have reading notebooks and we have a mini-lesson planned, but a child asks to use sticky notes instead, we had to truly evaluate why that would not be an acceptable choice.

Over the last several years, we've realized how our plans often get in the way of student choice. So, we've changed our planning (and our own expectations) to always give children true choice. To do this, we must think about the goal of the lesson, and then we must be committed to being open to students using whatever tools they feel will be most helpful for them.

We have come to realize that true choice is not a choice between two things that we, as the teachers, decide is appropriate. For true choice to happen, our students must have access to all the tools all the time.

Tools Are Everywhere!

A dry-erase table is a powerful tool for any classroom. Having access to a table invites collaborative thinking and problem-solving.

Tools can live in many areas of the room. We want as much time as possible to be dedicated to learning, and we certainly don't want a child to become frustrated and disengaged because they can't find their pen or pencil. Our goal with tools is to have them be as convenient as possible so that accessing the tools students may need at any moment is not a barrier to learning.

When it comes to community supplies, our goal is access. But that does not mean we don't also support individuals having their own supplies. Sometimes a child has a set of pencils that they received as a birthday present, or we have students who simply prefer to have their own tools. We are committed to the idea that community supplies can be a both/and situation. Tools are available to the community around the room AND students can have their own set of tools in their drawers or pencil pouches.

Our Must-Have Tools

- Markers, crayons, and pencils (including Crayola Colors of the World)
- Pens (various colors)
- Felt-tip pens
- Highlighters
- Sticky notes (various shapes and sizes)
- Clipboards
- Individual dry-erase boards
- Dry-erase markers
- Paint and paintbrushes
- Laptops or devices
- Staplers
- Hole punch and 3-hole punch
- Paper clips
- Headphones (individual)
- Pencil sharpeners
- Notebooks
- Paper
- Chart paper

Reading notebooks give students an easy way to jot down notes.

A variety of tools are available in all spaces, so students always have what they need at their fingertips. We don't want them to spend time looking for a pencil.

Laptops are always available for students. They choose a laptop to use in the same way they might choose a marker. Children are free to choose the best tool for the learning.

For our younger learners, having access to a variety of alphabet tools in various places around the room is important. Primary teachers Mary Brothers and Jessica Ardela have tools available throughout the room.

Young children are very intentional about their use of tools, and they often choose to use several tools at once to serve the purpose at hand.

Most of our learning tools are in easy-to-move containers. Having several sets of the same tools in portable containers allow children to grab a set and take it to their current learning space.

Every tool in the classroom is available to every student. Sometimes, this dry-erase board on wheels is used by the teacher in whole-group instruction. At other times, a small group or an individual student will pull the dry-erase board to their current spot to support their learning.

Felt-tip pens are a popular tool that Lynsey recently discovered. Having a variety of colors invites students to use the colors for different purposes. The fine tip allows flair pens to be used in a variety of ways (e.g., writing, drawing, annotating).

Our learners need access to staplers, paper, three-hole punches, and more!

Students have access to any calendars or event lists that are relevant. This student is signing up to read a book to the class.

All supplies are always available to students, even paints and paintbrushes.

Thinking about room design so that students have access to all tools, including digital tools, is important. Having tools available for students to share learning with the whole class means setting up the classroom with that in mind.

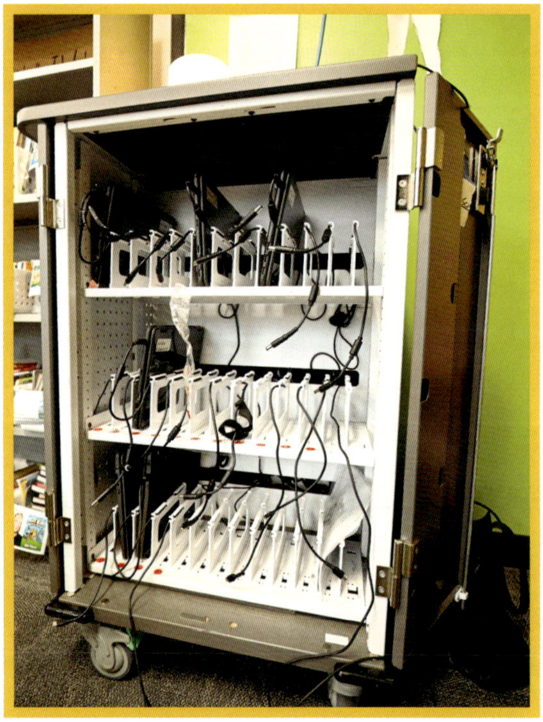

When we have a class set of laptops available, we can assign a student a numbered computer and space so they can access it as needed.

All learning tools are placed in spots that make them easy to access. These clipboards are always available to first graders.

Some classrooms always have pencil sharpeners available. Others have already sharpened pencils available, as well as a place to put unsharpened pencils so they can all be sharpened together at a convenient time.

The Role of Technology in Room Design

One year, Franki entered her room at the end of summer to find two new Apple computers had arrived. She was excited that students would have access to these in the classroom, but the arrival of these computers limited what she could do with the space. The computers were large; they had to be placed on the table that came with them, and they had to be connected to the network port in the wall. There were no options as to where the computers could go.

> "We cannot talk about room environment and student agency without including digital tools in the conversation."

A similar thing happened when our district installed SMART® Boards in every classroom. Over the summer, these were installed with connected projectors. The placement and height of the SMART® Boards could not be moved, so this was another area to navigate around when designing a classroom.

For a few years, we struggled because we often had to design our rooms around the placement of the technology. We wanted our interactive board to be available for things like read-alouds and mini-lessons, but the placement of the boards was often front and center rather than in a corner, which would be a better space for whole-class meetings.

As we navigated the placement of these new tools, we also learned ways to embed them into the classroom so they were not something separate. We asked to have them lowered or moved to a different area of the room. Laptops replaced large desktop computers, and much of the technology we have today is smaller and more portable.

We cannot talk about room environment and student agency without including digital tools in the conversation. We agree strongly with the words of Dr. Detra Price-Dennis and Dr. Selna Carrion in their 2017 *Language Arts* article when they say, "As literacy teachers who draw from culturally relevant and responsive approaches to teaching (Gay, 2000; Ladson-Billings, 1995; Nieto & Bode, 2008), we firmly believe in the need to incorporate our students' funds of knowledge (Gonzáles, Moll & Amanti, 2005) and vast literacy experiences in our practice. This includes centering digital tools in the curriculum to ensure opportunities to work with a variety of print-based and digital modalities and platforms."

Digital Tools for Student Agency

Just as with everything else in our classrooms, we think about technology with a lens toward student agency. Over the years, the digital tools have become more naturally embedded in all we do, so we intentionally think about the role of technology and digital tools as we think about room design.

It took us a few years to think about digital tools in the same ways we think about books, sticky notes, and markers — as one tool for learners. NCTE's *Definition of Literacy in a Digital Age* (2019) helped us think about the importance of access, choice, and intentionality when embedding digital tools into our classrooms:

> Learners have access to a wide variety of texts and tools. We engage with many multimedia texts in our daily lives for a variety of reasons. These texts not only give learners new information but also allow us to see our worlds in new ways. Engaging with texts that vary in format, genre, and medium gives us new perspectives and insights. Having knowledge and understanding of the various texts and tools available is important for using them intentionally. Being literate means making choices and using texts and tools in ways that match purpose. It also means thinking about texts and tools in new ways.

If you have student access to Chromebooks, iPads, laptops, or any device that connects to the internet in your classroom, you may have wondered at some point (or are still wondering), what is the best way to utilize these devices to support student learning and growth? We want our students to be agentive in all aspects of our classroom, and technology is another way to support student agency. We see devices as another tool for learning, and we see digital spaces as extensions of the classroom walls.

Our students have complete access to all the digital tools and spaces. This includes the interactive white board, the document camera, the laptops, and the mobile devices.

Choice Is Key

Both Franki and Lynsey vividly remember the years when our district implemented a Bring Your Own Device policy. Students could bring their own devices to the classroom every day. We knew that some children would have devices, and maybe some would not, and we knew that there would be different devices — some Android and some Apple devices. Each of these devices would have various apps, likely some that we both would be unfamiliar with.

We had many design conversations about what the environment would look like, both physically and digitally. We

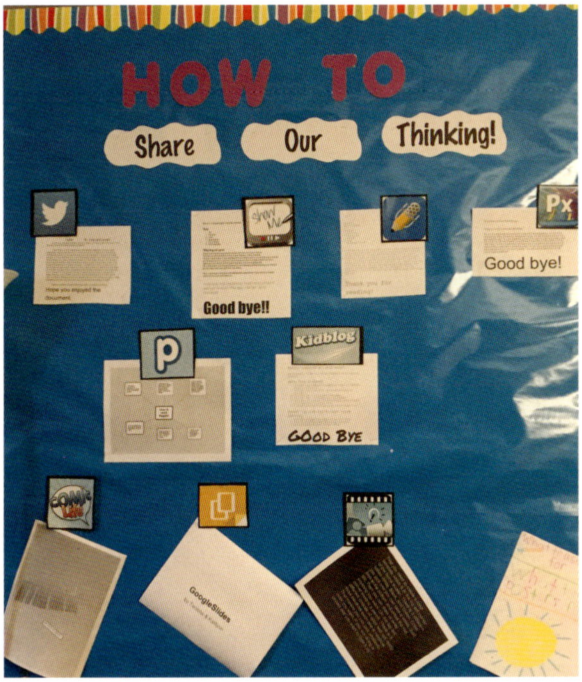

Early in the school year, third-grade teacher Kami Wenning created this board to remind students of the tools they had used and some tools that were available to them in their online classroom. Some of these were apps that the class used collaboratively (with the teacher as the model), and others were available for individual use. Creating a board like this together is helpful in valuing choice and purpose.

each decided that our digital environment had to be web-based so that any device could access the content. For us, that meant using Google tools and web-based applications such as Padlet, Epic (books), and Kindle. From this decision, we could really begin to think about the design of the digital space.

It is easy, when focusing on management, to limit children's choice with technology. But with a focus on student agency, we knew that limiting choice went against all we were trying to create in our classroom. So instead of limiting choice, we embraced it. The digital classroom and the applications just added more choices for our learners.

Interactive Board/Screen

Since our first SMART® Board was installed in our classrooms all those years ago, we have thought about how to best use it. We have seen many teachers use the board for lunch count, announcements, and more. That is one way to use the board, but we wanted the board, like the other digital tools in our classrooms, to be seen and utilized as a tool for learning.

The current interactive board in Lynsey's classroom is on wheels and connects wirelessly to devices in the classroom. (This is a far stretch from starting her first year of teaching with an overhead projector and a

Whatever is projected on the interactive board as part of a mini-lesson or student sharing can be put into the online classroom for student access at any time.

screen.) One commonality between the interactive board and the overhead projector is that both these devices show something in a projected way to a group of people. Because technology has evolved, we can now have students digitally share their reading and writing, annotate an ebook together, craft a digital piece as a group, search for information as a class, revise a piece of writing together, share writing using the document camera, and whatever else the reading and writing community wants to do with one another around the interactive board. Each day, students can choose where to sit in relation to the board.

Digital Charts and Access Outside of the Classroom

Because we want what we share on the interactive board to give more opportunities to our learners, we utilize Google Slides as digital anchor charts for reading, writing, math, and content. Just like anchor charts that hang on the wall, these digital charts hold the learning of the group during whole group instruction. With digital tools, students can now access these digital charts from home or at times when the whole class is not engaged with them. By using Padlet boards, Google Docs, or Slides, students are able to access and utilize these accessibility tools that come with their school accounts at any time.

As a mini-lesson is taking place, Lynsey can co-facilitate conversation and learning with students and type the students' thoughts, wonderings, and assertions on the slides in real time. Many times, students are not ready to share or time doesn't allow for everyone's contribution, so they are invited to add their comments to the slides during independent learning time.

Students always take this opportunity! The Google Slides are available in the Google Classroom, so not only do students always have access, but parents can also see in real time and in the evenings alongside their students what is happening during our mini-lessons.

Note: Lynsey does not have a slide deck of mini-lessons ready to start each unit; Instead, these slides truly serve as anchor charts only and are developed together with her students during mini-lesson time. When a new unit begins, the slides only have a title slide with the name of the unit, individual slides with the curriculum standards they will be covering, and the initial slide to kick off the learning. This initial slide is a book cover with a student quote next to it that goes along with the unit they will be engaging with in reading, writing, math, or content.

Intentional Design of Online Classroom

The document camera, along with the interactive board, gives students the opportunity to share reading with the class to build understanding.

We learned quickly that a well-designed and simple learning management system is the key to allowing students ownership over the space. The LMS could provide a digital space for learning to take place in the classroom or beyond that single space.

Whatever learning management platform you use, consider making it simple so that students can easily navigate it and find ways to insert their voices. In Lynsey's Google Classroom there are five topics: Reading Workshop, Writing Workshop, Math

In the years that we've had a laptop for each student, it is easy for someone to grab a laptop as a tool when needed. It is very seldom that every child is using a laptop at the same time.

Workshop, Word Study, and Content. Under each topic is a link to the Google Slides, websites students feel are helpful during the unit, and links to the text sets students are studying during whole-group instruction. Students use the stream page to share links to their digital work, to say hello, or pass on something to share with the class.

We like learning management sites that are intuitive for students to navigate, sites where sharing links and posting shared material (by both teacher and students) is quick and simple. We look for sites to have places where students can comment and add links to their work — this allows for an extended or digital wall space!

Quality Opportunities

We are always asking ourselves these questions to ensure students have quality opportunities with the digital environment:

1. Are students part of the digital design discussion?
2. Are students making suggestions about how to better use a digital tool or ways other digital tools could work for what they are doing?
3. How often are students creating versus consuming?
4. Do students interact with each other in the digital space?
5. Are students able to choose to use a digital tool for learning when they see it is the best tool for the purpose?
6. Do students have access to digital tools in the same ways they have access to other learning tools?
7. Can students access digital spaces and resources outside of the classroom and the school day?
8. Do students have the opportunity to create and curate as part of their learning?

Book Bins as a Tool for Student Agency

Years ago, Franki realized that her third graders would finish a book and then stand at the bookshelf with no idea what to read next. She thought about her own reading life and realized this never happened to her because she always had many books on her nightstand — she was always looking for books she might want to read in the future.

As readers, many of us have next-read stacks. Whether these are physical stacks or titles we keep on a list or in our heads, we are always thinking ahead. Book bins are a tangible way for young readers to begin thinking ahead as readers. It gives them a physical place to put books that they want to read soon. This isn't a commitment, so readers can change their minds about what to read next. Instead, book bins become a place to practice thinking ahead as a reader. These bins came out of a need to support readers in building their next read stacks, and they have grown from there. We've found that individual book bins are a teaching tool for readers at all levels.

One year, Franki noticed several fifth graders were quitting books in the middle and moving on to another. While we are supportive of a reader abandoning a book when it ends up not being a good match, if quitting becomes a default or a habit for a reader, we must dig a bit deeper into the reasons.

When Franki met with students to ask about why they were quitting so many books, she discovered an interesting pattern. They weren't quitting because they weren't engaged in the books; instead, many of the readers would see or hear about another book that diverted their attention. Since they did not have practice in building a next-read stack, they quit the current book and started the new one. Franki helped these readers see that the book bin allowed them to finish the book they were reading without the worry of forgetting about the book they were excited to read next. The book bin served as a scaffold to change habits.

> “When Franki met with students to ask about why they were quitting so many books, she discovered an interesting pattern. They weren't quitting because they weren't engaged in the books; instead, many of the readers would see or hear about another book that diverted their attention. Since they did not have practice in building a next-read stack, they quit the current book and started the new one. Franki helped these readers see that the book bin allowed them to finish the book they were reading without the worry of forgetting about the book they were excited to read next. The book bin served as a scaffold to change habits.”

As one of the first mini-lessons of the year, our readers fill their book bins with a few books they might like to read. This introduces readers to the idea of the book bin and thinking ahead as readers. It also gives them a first invitation to explore the classroom library and talk about their reading tastes and preferences. These are the three books Blair chose for her book bin on the first day of fifth grade.

Many readers use their book bins to hold themselves to reading more than one kind of book. So, they might decide to always have a nonfiction or poetry title in their bin along with a fiction chapter book. And we always have readers who prefer to read more than one book at a time or who have the stamina to stick with a single book for a longer amount of time than is allotted in the classroom. Their book bins become a place to hold things like magazines, poetry, or books with stand-alone pages to read when they have short spurts of time. We also find readers who become interested in a certain topic or genre, and their bin becomes a space to house the text set they create on that topic. One student became interested in picture book biographies of athletes in history, so he filled his bin with that kind of book for weeks.

Book bins increase engagement during independent reading time. They allow readers to think about the books they want to read and to "shop" for books they can read in the coming days. Filled bins ensure that they have plenty of books to keep them reading during independent reading time without having to get up to find a book. By giving readers time to fill their bins, we give them time to think about their needs as readers and to take the time needed to find books without cutting into reading time. Book bins give readers a tangible way to think about and talk about their reading life. From naming the types of books they are looking for to reflecting to discovering strategies for finishing books, bins are a powerful teaching tool.

Help Readers Curate Book Bins

Book bins have become a great resource when conferring with readers. We often have readers bring their bins to the conference and begin the conversation there. Some questions we ask to get started include:

- What is in your book bin? Why did you choose these books?
- Are you in the mood to stick with texts like the ones you've been reading, or are you hoping to expand the things you read?
- Are you finishing most of the books that you start?
- How will you decide what to read next?
- What strategies did you use for choosing the books in your bin?
- Is there anything you are thinking about as a future reader that I can help you with?

Blair with her book bin at her side, ready for independent reading time.

Book bins typically house books and reading notebooks. Sometimes, students include sticky notes and writing devices. The bins are portable, so when a child is ready to read, they can grab their bin and find a reading spot.

Students browse all areas of the classroom library to fill their book bins.

Just as our classroom libraries are not in one location in the classroom, student book bins are located around the room. Before the school year begins, we find the places where a small number of book bins can live, and they are then ready for students to fill.

Placing the bins in various spots around the room helps with management and traffic.

Working with the Space You Have

Lynsey's first glance from the front door immediately drew her eyes to all the storage opportunities. Cabinets lined the entire left side of the irregularly shaped room. The room almost felt like it was divided into two separate sections.

In June of 2017, Lynsey was preparing to teach second grade in a new building and a new classroom. Designing a classroom where students were able to read, write, think, compute, share, research, and form a community was at the center of her thoughts. Like many teachers, she couldn't see the space she would be teaching in until late June of that year. Mid-August was the start date of the new school year, so she knew she had to have a plan for the space that could be implemented quickly but with a design such that the space could grow with the community. She knew the room was not originally designed as a classroom space, so she would have to be thoughtful about how to make it feel like a space where students were empowered as learners.

The day Lynsey first entered the space, she quickly took note of what the space offered. Designing a room for student agency meant that Lynsey needed to find space where the class could come together for whole-group instruction. Students would also need a classroom library that was distributed throughout the room, so they were not always headed to one space to browse for books. In addition to these spaces, there would need to be a space for art supplies, book bins, writing folders, word study journals, and Chromebooks.

There was the carpeted section and a hard-floored section—the spaces had, in fact, previously been used as the school's literacy resource and intervention room. Lynsey thought about how she was going to merge the two spaces to feel like one cohesive unit for her twenty incoming second-grade students.

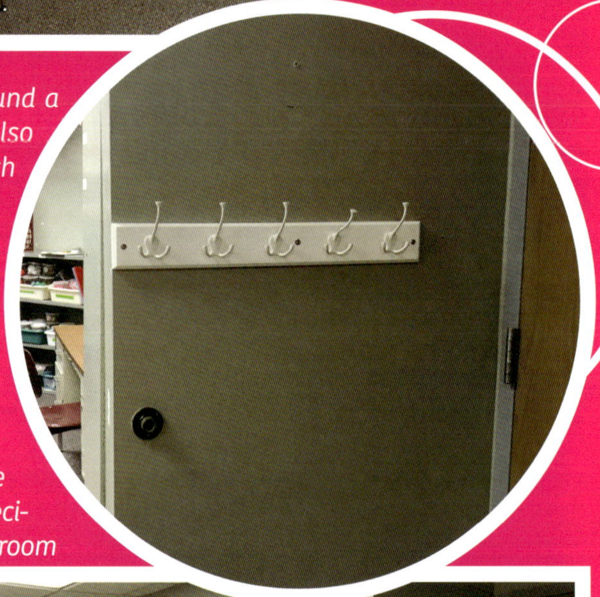

As Lynsey continued to examine the room, she found a tiny coat hook that reminded her that there would also need to be spaces for coats, backpacks, and lunch boxes. This hook was certainly not sufficient!

The space had a traditional teacher's desk and tables with undermount storage for students' materials. There were high and low bookshelves that had belonged to the literacy resource room. Lynsey also wondered how second graders would access the taller bookshelves safely. She had to make some decisions as to how she was going to free up space in a room that wasn't meant to be a classroom. There were also too many tables in the room. For students to be able to sit at traditional tables or lie on the floor or cozy up in a corner of the room, there would need to be fewer traditional tables. In considering how this classroom should look, Lynsey knew the teacher desk would not stay.

Leave Space for Student Work on the Walls

Don't forget the storage! These wall cabinets presented endless possibilities. Storage is important in elementary classrooms—we have indoor recess toys, learning materials, and teacher resources to house. Lynsey had to think about what the essentials were going to be for the classroom in determining how the existing storage should be used.

Looking at the walls, Lynsey immediately knew that less is more so that student work could be centered on those surfaces. She also understood that she would have no use for old maps and projection screens. All those things could be taken down, along with any charts left over from the previous use of the space.

A smaller TV did not directly support students' use of the room. It was there, but how might the students engage with it? An important aspect of agentive classrooms is that what is in the rooms is centered around how students might use those items to support their literacy journeys. The whiteboard was essential because both students and teacher could use it as part of the learning process.

Essential Spaces

Following are what, over the years, we have come to consider to be essential spaces in a classroom for the different kinds of learning we want to see taking place:

- Whole-group space
- Classroom library
- Partner spaces
- Small-group spaces
- Flexibility
- Wall space

The cabinets were cleared out to make room for the classroom essentials:

- *Book bins*
- *Writing folders and word study journals*
- *Coats and backpacks*
- *Art supplies*
- *Technology*

Garage sale finds with fresh coats of paint resulted in pieces that can humanize the room and make it feel more inviting. Low coffee tables allow for students to have space for conversation. A kitchen table provides a round seating option for small groups to face each other while working.

Classroom Library around the Room

Storage Fixes

Book bins line the countertop, and the white boxes hold art supplies so students can grab whatever they need. The bottom cabinets are empty and have enough space to fit students' coats and backpacks. Twelve Chromebooks were stored on top of the counter. Pencils were spread out around the room so students could easily access them regardless of where they were in the room.

The tall cabinet toward the back of the room held learning manipulatives, indoor recess games, and more art supplies. The shelves at the top that students could not reach were used to store teacher curricular materials and files.

There was plenty of flexible furniture. The small white tables could be moved out of the way, and the gray benches were on sliders so they could be quickly pushed to make way for whole-group instruction. The tall, white tables toward the back have wheels for more flexibility. The white board was lowered so students could reach it. A large TV allowed for connectivity with computers for whole-group instruction and so students could share from their Chromebooks.

Wall space was left mostly blank so students could use it to make their learning visible throughout the school year.

Over the years, we have found ways to work in the spaces we are given. We've also learned to ask around to see if there are pieces of furniture we can swap out. We've also learned to:

- Ask whether there is a central warehouse with extra stored items. We visit the warehouse if we can. Sometimes we are not sure what we want but when we see something, we see the possibilities.
- Swap furniture with other teachers.
- Visit garage sales for small pieces of furniture and learning tools. One or two nontraditional pieces invites new ways of thinking for our students.
- Repurpose the furniture we already have.
- Ask about adding wheels to traditional school furniture. Often, our custodians have wheels that can easily be added to tables and desks.
- Think about using traditional furniture in new ways. Dropping a traditional table to a low level so that students can sit on the floor provides flexibility. Can you create different seating options by raising or lowering tables and desks?
- Use traditional desks and tables in nontraditional ways. Try having some desks in clusters while others are placed individually against the wall.
- Pay attention to the ways students find to use the space and build from that. One year, Franki's third graders began using the large cubby areas (intended to store coats and bookbags) as working spaces. They'd clear out the supplies and have a quiet area to work. It was easy to find new places for storage so that these cubbies could become more permanent options for student seating.
- If you must keep a teacher's desk, file cabinet, or kidney table, think about how those can be repurposed. Can the teacher's desk be transformed into a student work space? Can the side of the file cabinet be used for students to jot down thinking using sticky notes and magnets? Can the kidney table be pushed against a wall to invite a different type of grouping?

As educators, many of us walk into spaces that we have no control over and are told to teach in them. What we do have control over is working within that space to design with a focus on student agency.

The classroom is finally ready for students.

Working with the Furniture You Have

We like the message of a kitchen table rather than a kidney table, as it is meant to bring people together.

We have taught in a variety of schools. We've taught in new schools where teachers could choose their own furniture, and we've taught in old schools where every classroom had a desk for each student. We've worked in schools where principals allowed us to bring in our own furniture, and we've worked in schools where we were required to use only the furniture that was already in the classroom. We've worked in schools where we could get rid of unneeded furniture or furniture that didn't work for us, and we've worked in schools where every classroom was required to have the same furniture, regardless of whether it worked for the children. We've worked in schools where the fire marshal didn't allow much on the walls, and we've worked in schools where we had full control of the wall space. We've both been in large, spacious rooms, and we've both been in small rooms with irregular shapes. We've been in rooms with lots of light and windows, and we've been in rooms with no windows at all.

Somehow, we've made every room work. We admit that some years, it was easier than others to navigate the space, furniture, and school rules. Looking back on all the rooms in which each of us has taught, regardless of constraints, we were focused on the messages about learning that each space sent to our students. And no matter the constraints, we could create flexibility via large-group spaces and spaces for small-group and individual work. We could create spaces where students' learning and students' words were amplified and visible.

We have found that furniture placement in a classroom sends strong messages, and often the furniture and placement of furniture send the misguided message that we value compliance over learning. In her article, "On Kidney Tables: Small Changes for Big Effects" (Choice Literacy), Principal Karen Szymusiak shares her thinking when deciding to purchase round tables instead of kidney-shaped ones for the new elementary school she would be leading:

> I began thinking about the kidney table and imagining what it feels like to sit there as a child. I wondered if children feel less responsible for their own learning as they wait to be directed by the teacher sitting on the other side of the table. Our school will be a place for the children. The school belongs to every child and not to the adults who work there every day. The school should be a place that promotes collaborative and interactive learning with many thoughtful conversations about learning. Can that happen at a kidney table? We think not, because the design sets the teacher up as the all-knowing authority who is taller, bigger, and smarter than those sitting on the other side.

Questions We Ask Ourselves

When Setting Up a New Space:

- What opportunities do I see here? What are the positives about this space?
- What are the biggest challenges in this classroom?
- How can I look at the space with fresh eyes?
- How can I design the space to create a variety of spaces for learning?
- How can I use the furniture in creative ways?
- Which spaces in the room will be most important? (Tip: Create those first!)
- How can I make the space flexible so that students can determine for themselves how to use it?
- Can wheels be added to any of the furniture?

We have discovered that we can make any space work if we remember our goal of student agency. If we are forced to keep a kidney table in the room, we make sure it is not the table we use for small-class instruction. If we have individual desks, we think about various configurations that allow for various learning spaces in the classroom. When wall space is limited, we use digital spaces in new ways.

We take advantage of small spaces and make room for individual or small groups of students by using smaller furniture.

We can use traditional school furniture and drop it to a lower height level and use floor pillows instead of chairs for a more comfortable, homey feel. Using the furniture we have in innovative ways gives students choices in how they use the space.

What Is Good Here?

This section of the room had multiple spaces for small groups to gather, could be moved for a large gathering, and had an interactive screen.

One winter afternoon, a group of third graders in Lynsey's classroom decided that a particular round table and section of the room worked well for small-group writing share time. During the Writers' Workshop, these students wanted a place to gather and quickly share what they were working on without interrupting the work of other writers who preferred a quiet environment. This space worked, but it didn't remain that way for the rest of the year as students changed things as other needs arose. At the beginning of the year, we set up our rooms to create space for student agency. As the year progresses, we (students and teacher alike) make changes collaboratively based on all we see that works well and not so well.

We know there are times when we want to rearrange our classrooms, such as when we notice students using spaces in ways we never imagined. We notice the ways groups work within the space we created. Some things are working, but sometimes there are things that aren't working, and we know changes will help. Typically, big redesigns happen at the start of the school year and during winter break. But when we think about classroom design that supports free living, we always go back to a question stance we learned from Carla Shalaby in her book *Troublemakers*: "What is good here?"

Asking "What is good here?" allows us to build upon the strengths of the community. Rather than starting all over with the design of your classroom when the room doesn't seem to be working or when you are getting ready to begin a new school year, pause, look around, and ask, "What is good here?" When we started to ask this question, we began to think of our students in the classroom space differently.

One year, as Lynsey was preparing the classroom space in late July, she walked the room asking herself this question. She arranged furniture and spaces and then looked at the spaces asking herself, "What is good here?"

We know there is more than one right way to set up any classroom, so Lynsey knew this design was just one option of what the room could be. She needed the students to truly make the space work for the needs of the community. Once school started, the room changed. It was a slow change, but it gradually started to develop into what the students needed.

This space has:

- *Labeled book bins*
- *Spaces for partner work*
- *Books spread around the room*
- *Screens for sharing work via Chromebook*

There are small individual tables where students can work and move around the room to other spaces. There are also soft options for floor seating, and students can make choices about the types of spaces they want to use.

Changing in Response to Needs

Early in the year, the two white tables on wheels in the meeting area moved to another part of the room. The class had decided it took too much time to move them out of the way, and they wanted a large open space to work during independent reading and writing times.

The bookshelves also moved. They were too tall, and students used the library better when there were shorter options, which helped with browsing and quick book finds. Children were not able to access the higher shelves, so Lynsey replaced the bookshelves.

Classrooms where the spaces are fluid allow students and the teacher to make room for needs that might quickly arise but also quickly evolve into something else. Some questions to help break down the question of "What is good here?" and to reflect on whether the classroom is agentive, free-living, identity-building, and community-centered include:

- Are the tools that readers and writers need at their fingertips, or are they put away for the teacher to get out?
- Does the space meet the physical needs of the students? Are learning tools easily accessible for every child?
- Is there flexibility for student decision-making over the spaces in the classroom?
- Are the tables and chairs set up for multiple groupings of learning and conversation?
- Are there opportunities for students to create new spaces as needed?
- Who owns the wall space?
- Could a visitor walk in and see the personality of the community and individuals reflected in the space?
- Whose voice is predominant in the physical setup of the furniture in your space?
- What types of materials dominate your space?

We know now as teachers that we can only imagine the spaces we know should be available if we want our students to use them to support their learning. By asking ourselves, "What is good here?" as we are designing our classrooms, we can create an arrangement that establishes a good beginning. It isn't until the entire community arrives that the space then becomes the third teacher of the community.

Part 2

The Classroom Library

The Importance of a Robust Classroom Library

In this primary classroom, books are embedded in each area of the classroom instead of being in one single area.

Every child deserves to be in a classroom with a robust classroom library in which all their identities are represented. Classroom libraries should support students as readers and as whole human beings, inviting them and supporting them in choosing their own books.

Curating a classroom library is one of the most important jobs we have as teachers. However, curation is just the first step in building a classroom library that supports growing readers. Intentional design is as critical to our young readers as offering a collection of diverse, quality books. When curated and organized thoughtfully, our classroom libraries can be the anchor for our readers' learning and growing, allowing students to see themselves as readers and take ownership of finding books for themselves. The classroom library can be a teacher of readers.

The Classroom Library Is NOT a Location

The classroom library is not in a single space in Lynsey's third-grade classroom. Instead, the room is designed so that the classroom library is a part of each area.

We don't think of the classroom library as a separate area of the classroom. Instead, it should be spread out throughout the space and intentionally woven into the design of the entire classroom. This brings us back to the point of creating a coffee shop feel.

The Classroom Library Is Responsive to Students

There is no one way to organize the classroom library. We have each taught various grades, and each year, we have a new group of readers. So, our classroom library is never quite the same. And we know when we set up the library each year, it will evolve based on the community that lives and learns in it.

We want books to be accessible to children, so the Otis books are organized on this low shelf for young readers.

Classroom Library as Collective Curation

We view classroom library curation as a partnership between students and the teacher. We call this collective curation: The library evolves because the community has collective input on what is added and how books are grouped and displayed. The students and the teacher are viewed as co-curators. This thinking is based on the work of Paolo Freire and his idea of co-constructing learning between students and the teacher. Lynsey remembers a recent conversation with a student:

Carter: Mrs. Burkins, I was looking at some of the books that were on my bookmoji recommendation list, and I think there are some books we should have in our classroom.

Lynsey: Ooh Carter let me see! (Lynsey walks over to Carter's computer and looks at the Bookelicious website on his screen. Bookelicious is an online bookstore for children that specializes in matching books with readers.)

Carter: See, some of these books we have, but all these we don't. (Carter is pointing to his screen.) I think other kids would like these too.

Lynsey: What do you think we should do?

Carter: Maybe we can make a list and ask other kids if they want to add.

Lynsey: Ok, I'll let you take charge!

This was a quick conversation between Carter and Lynsey, but it led to students creating a list and Lynsey's principal ordering books. This is just a small example of an everyday conversation that is rooted in collective curation.

Collective curation looks like students having time to get to know themselves as readers so that they are able to articulate what type of books they would like to see in their classroom library. When students know their reading identities, they are able to better say what they think is missing in the library and what they think should be displayed.

Collective curation also looks like students having time to browse the classroom library, read from books that are part of the classroom library, and most importantly, talk together about the books in the classroom library. This community approach adds to the collective knowledge of what books the classroom library contains and what the reading community thinks they need.

Collective curation can look like students having access to empty bins to create book collections of their own or highlighting books they want their fellow reading community to read. Students also know they have the ability to make labels and create displays of books based on their ideas of how books could be grouped and sorted. This type of classroom library curation is done as a collective.

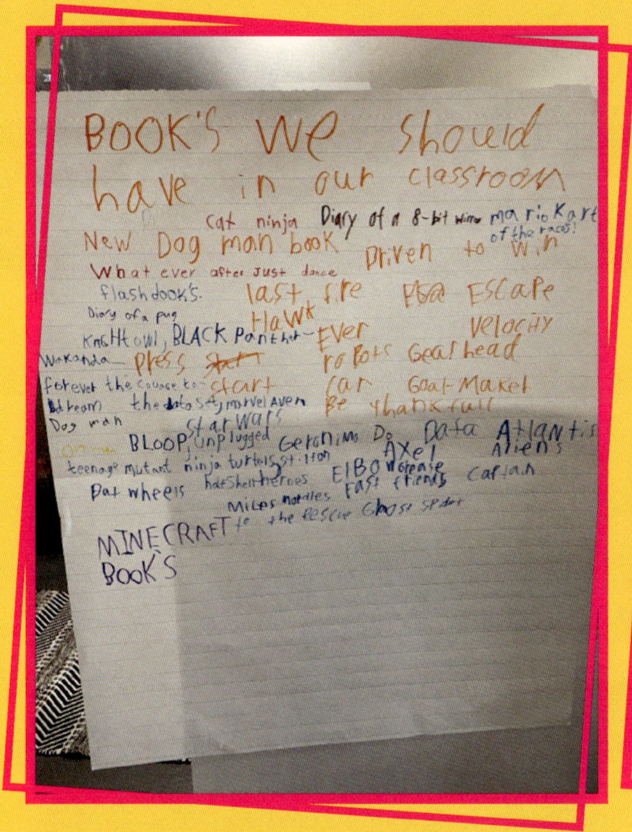

A classroom-created list of books students want in the classroom library.

Leaving space in bins allows for new books to be added or co-curated collections to grow.

Readers getting to know the classroom library together.

Agency, Reader Identity, and the Classroom Library

Over the years, we have both written about the intentional organization of our classroom libraries as a way for our readers to find books and to engage as readers. But as we've learned more about the power of classroom design to act as the third teacher, we have learned that our library design also serves as a teacher itself. For us, a good classroom library is far more than a place where readers choose books. The goal of our libraries is to support readers as they build agency, identity, and skills as readers. It is in the process of choosing books that students come to know themselves as readers and begin to have agency as readers.

As their choices of books expand and their skills as readers grow, their identity and agency also grow. Our classroom libraries help students know themselves deeply as growing and changing readers.

In Franki's fifth-grade classroom, books are organized in various ways throughout the classroom. The labels on the baskets help readers think about strategies for finding new books. Some are also placed strategically with materials connected to the kinds of thinking those books might connect to, such as math picture books with math manipulatives.

The Classroom Library as Teaching Tool

When the classroom library is curated and designed intentionally, it becomes a teaching tool. Not only can we learn about our readers daily as they interact with the classroom library, but we can also learn about them through conversations anchored in the classroom library.

The library becomes an important tool in our classroom for recommending books, reflecting on reading, getting to know new authors, studying a writer's craft, and more. It allows us, as teachers, to learn about our readers continuously throughout the year.

Classroom Library Design Is Ongoing and Responsive

Knowing our students as readers and supporting them in knowing themselves as readers is an ongoing process. This work often starts with beginning-of-the-year reading interviews, etc., but the classroom library can continue to be a place where students learn about who they are and who they might become as readers. Just as reader identity is not something we focus on only at the beginning of the school year, classroom library curation and design is also ongoing. As Aeriale Johnson writes in her brilliant May 2022 *Language Arts* article, "Interrogating Classroom Libraries: From Diversity to Responsiveness and Inclusion":

> A responsively inclusive classroom library should not be static. Instead, it should be a part of our learning community that is so dynamic that it comes alive and walks alongside us — educators and children — as we grow our capacity to be readers who are skillful, intellectual, and vulnerable enough to be galvanized to become more compassionate human beings through our transaction with texts.

There are many ways to organize books into baskets in this primary classroom. There are baskets that serve as mentor texts for writers ("How-To" and "Opinion"), baskets based on a topic of interest ("Space"), and baskets of "Family Stories." This variety begins to teach readers the different reasons we may choose a book at a certain time.

Curation and Design vs. Management

We spend almost no time thinking about the management of book checkout, how readers will put books away, or how we will keep track of the books that students borrow for home reading. We believe that a quality classroom library is about being responsive to readers and the classroom community.

We don't typically label books in the classroom library; instead, we label baskets and areas of the classroom library to support readers in finding books and reflecting on ways they are choosing books. Because the library changes a bit each year, anytime we have labeled books, we have had to relabel them the next year based on our revisions. More important, we find that when students think about where to put a book back when they are finished, rather than looking at a label and matching it to a book basket, they do the thinking as readers and how readers sometimes categorize reading.

> "We don't typically label books in the classroom library; instead, we label baskets and areas of the classroom library to support readers in finding books and reflecting on ways they are choosing books."

There are many baskets that make sense for a particular book, so there is not often a single correct place for a book. It can be put in the series basket it is a part of, in the basket of new books, or in an area of mentor texts for writing. Because our libraries are fluid, the ways in which readers choose the books is varied, and we don't want to take that thinking piece away, as we believe the skills learned are worth losing track of a few books here and there.

We know that access to books is important for every student, and as NCTE reminds us in its Statement on Classroom Libraries, ". . . when students possess the skills necessary to access, select, use, and effectively evaluate their reading materials, their ability to become engaged members of their communities and productive citizens is enhanced." So, our libraries are designed for matching readers to books, but just as important, for helping readers build skills and agency as they learn to select their own books.

Curating a Diverse Classroom Library

Curating a diverse classroom library takes time and energy. It is also a commitment. We have spent a lot of time thinking about and learning from the infographic created by Sarah Park Dahlen and David Huyck on page 108 that is based on statistics compiled by the Cooperative Children's Book Center.

We understand that because of power and privilege, the representation of stories that are about and told by the global majority are not being published at the same rate as stories about lived experiences that have not been minoritized. We also understand that power and privilege are given to white, male, straight, cis, Christian, able-bodied, land-owning lived experiences. We use the word *diverse* to indicate that contents of the library should be diverse from the identities that have power and privilege; this way, our classroom libraries are representative of the lived experiences we see in our world.

Chad Everett, in his piece "There Is No Diverse Book" (2017), explains, "Using the word 'diverse' to describe texts also creates a default position, because one must ask diverse for whom or diverse from what? The word diverse as it is currently used centers heteronormative whiteness as the default. We also lose sight of the big picture. Any diverse booklist would have to have a variety of races, abilities, gender, etc., represented. So, if you find yourself holding a booklist and notice that the creators have simply compiled a list of non-white authors, know that you are not holding a diverse book list."

He continues: "The call for diverse texts is a response to the overwhelming underrepresentation of individuals from minoritized groups as well as the underwhelming number of publishers publishing own voices, and this is laudable."

Dr. Rudine Sims Bishop's transformational work in 1990 has been an anchor for us as our classroom libraries have grown and evolved. Her work taught us that "Children need windows and mirrors. They need mirrors in which they see themselves and windows through which they see the world" ("Mirror, Windows and Sliding Glass Doors"). From her work, we learned the power of children seeing themselves and others represented in the books they read.

The infographic that follows on the next page makes visible the fact that there are not close to "enough" books being published with strong representations of characters from diverse backgrounds. But it is our job to make sure that our classroom libraries do NOT reflect these numbers. We can't use publishing problems as an excuse to not provide diverse classroom libraries to our students. Instead, we've made a strong commitment to reading widely, finding publishers we can trust, and listening to the voices of children's literature experts. We work to find every single book we can that depicts characters without the negative stereotypes or tropes we often see in books.

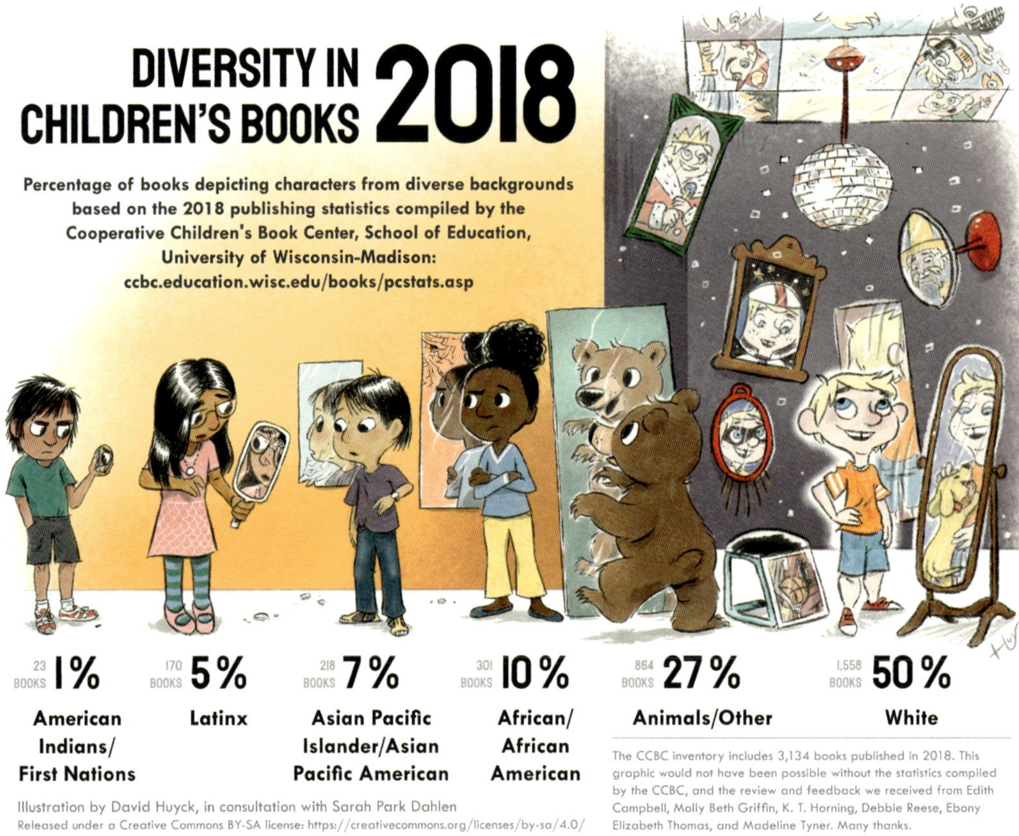

Diversity in Children's Literature, 2018.

We are not only interested in the number of books we have, but we are also committed to making sure that those books in our library have incidental diversity. We do not want a collection of books about the global majority that focus only on the struggle, oppression, and injustice endured. Instead, we want to make sure that our readers can see themselves and others in incidental ways. As Lynsey stated in a recent article, "While we do need books that teach us about injustices and histories of all people, we also need books that show communities of people experiencing the human experience of everyday life. Having both types of books prevents children from only seeing characters and people in one way.

For example, if students only saw Black characters in books that deal with racism, then some students may form inaccurate assumptions about a group of people. Incidental books allow for all children to see people and communities in ways that connect across the human experience." We work to discover new authors whose work may not be highlighted in large bookstores or who do not get the benefit of a huge marketing campaign when their books are published.

You can read more about incidental diversity in Lynsey's "Bring Me a Book" article here.

Curating and updating a quality, diverse classroom library takes time, energy, and a commitment from us as teachers. If we do not want our libraries to match the infographic; instead, we want every child to experience mirrors, windows, and sliding glass doors in the books they read, so we must commit to read widely, to actively search for new authors and publishers, and to learn from others who have expertise in diverse children's literature.

Of course, our students are key in helping us create our libraries. As Lynsey states in her piece "Classroom Library Audit" (*Game Changers*, 2018), "I always tell my students they should seek to find books in which they can see themselves. It is my responsibility to surround them with books allowing for this to happen." So over the years, we've shopped alongside students to add more bilingual and translanguaging books as well as books written in children's first languages to our library. We've added cookbooks when we realized students were bringing in cookbooks from home to read during Reading Workshop. And when students don't see themselves represented in books, we know we have to look beyond mainstream publishers. Our students are always suggesting books to add to the classroom, and they are instrumental in its ongoing curation.

We cannot create a library on our own, and we are thankful for everyone who shares their expertise to help us as teachers choose the best books for our students. Dr Laura Jiménez's article, "The Overwhelmingly White, Straight and Able Face of Children's Literature," outlines this in more depth. Jiménez also gives us a long list of resources to help us do this work in curating the classroom libraries our children deserve.

Following is a list of some of the resources we have relied on. This list is in no way comprehensive, of course, and we are always learning and finding new people who teach us and help us discover the best new books.

American Indians in Children's Literature

Founded by Dr. Debbie Reese, this is our go-to resource for books featuring Indigenous characters and those by Indigenous authors. For nearly twenty years, Reese has been more than generous in sharing her knowledge, and we have learned so much and discovered books with negative stereotypes that we would have missed without her expertise. We read her blog regularly and use her site to look up books that we are considering adding to our classroom library. We also use her blog to decide when to weed a book out.

Booktoss

Dr. Laura Jiménez's blog, Booktoss, has taught us how to read more critically. Jiménez is brilliant when looking closely at popular books to help us see negative stereotypes and tropes that we may otherwise miss.

We Need Diverse Books

We Need Diverse Books is a trusted website that we rely on for discovering new books and resources to build our classroom libraries as well as our own knowledge and understanding of books.

Latinx Kidlit Book Festival

This is a virtual annual event that celebrates Latinx kidlit books, authors, and illustrators. We love this event for all that it offers each year, but we've also learned so much and discovered so many new Latinx creators that the archived festivals have become one of our go-to resources for adding to our book lists.

The Brown Bookshelf

This a great resource for discovering Black authors. The site shares that it was "created by a group of authors and illustrators who came together to push awareness of the myriad of African American voices for young readers."

Lee and Low

This is one of the largest publishers of multicultural books and is a wonderful resource for discovering new books and authors.

Heartdrum

This is an imprint by Native American authors with a strong collection of books for K–8 readers.

Hijabi Librarians

Another favorite resource, this one is by a group of librarians who review books that feature Muslim characters and protagonists. The blog alone is an incredible resource. Additional resources on the site include a Book Release Calendar, various booklists, publisher recommendations, a toolkit for evaluating Muslims in kidlit, and more.

Social Justice Books

This is part of Teaching for Change. It reviews children's books and curates lists to help fill the gap that is present in so many classrooms and libraries.

Libros for Language

This is a new digital curation of translanguaging books. The books are browsable by language, genre, and grade level. As we strive to create libraries that include all languages, this site is an important one and looks to be one that will grow over time.

PJ Library

The main goal of this organization is to give books that celebrate Jewish values and culture to families. Their site has a section that recommends books.

Award Lists

Book award lists help us find new books, but more important, they help us discover new authors. When prizes are awarded from the American Library Association, the National Council of Teachers of English, and other organizations, we get to know the books on the list and then move onto checking out award-winning authors who are new to us. NCTE's Charlotte Huck Award, NCTE's Orbis Pictus Award, and the ALA Awards have introduced us to many #ownvoices books and new-to-us authors.

When we notice gaps in our classroom libraries, we can go to award lists like the Asian/Pacific American Award for Literature archived list to discover books and authors we've missed. That ensures that our students see themselves represented in the books in our classrooms and in the authors we choose, giving us the chance to create inclusive, welcoming environments.

The Classroom Library as a Teaching Tool

The books we display must be intentional. We change these out often, as many readers are drawn to books on display. Displays can be used to invite readers to try something new or to revisit an old favorite.

> *Children, just like adults, learn better in a supportive environment in which they can risk trying out new strategies and concepts and stretching themselves intellectually.*
>
> — Peter H. Johnston, *Choice Words* (2004)

Our classroom library collections are the hearts of our classrooms. We want our readers to find books they love, and we want them to fall in love with reading. We know that having access to a well-curated classroom library is an important step in supporting children as they become lifelong readers. But we also know that the ways in which we design our classroom libraries can do so much more than just connect children to books they will love. We believe we can do that and ensure that students grow in skills, strategies, and identities as readers. If designed intentionally, the classroom library as part of the environment can serve as the third teacher. The library design, in itself, can teach.

We want our readers to love books. That's a given. But we want them to love books, *and* we want them to grow as readers: to see themselves as readers who are capable and confident. We want them to know that they have choice and agency as readers, and we want them to be able to use the skills and strategies to grow and change as readers. Our libraries are designed to scaffold readers — where they are now and where they might grow.

Our libraries should support the kind of book choices that happen outside of school. Readers choose books in a variety of ways and for a variety of reasons. We are committed to ensuring that our students have authentic experiences as readers and that our classroom library design supports that.

> "Our libraries should support the kind of book choices that happen outside of school. Readers choose books in a variety of ways and for a variety of reasons. We are committed to ensuring that our students have authentic experiences as readers and that our classroom library design supports that."

With a well-designed classroom library, students grow in so many ways. They not only find books they love, but they also learn to identify as readers who are part of a reading community. They can begin to trust themselves to make decisions about what they read, based not only on their interests as readers but also with awareness that their tastes can change and that they can choose books for a variety of purposes.

As readers become comfortable choosing books in authentic ways, they learn to think about themselves in new ways. They may realize that "I am the kind of person who likes books by Kwame Alexander," or "I am the kind of reader who is starting to enjoy novels in verse," or "I am the kind of reader who is ready to try something new, and it might be historical fiction."

We think long and hard about the books we make visible and the messages the classroom library sends to students that very first time they walk into their new classroom. What they see in the classroom library can motivate or deflate young readers. We want every child to enter that room and see familiar characters they love and books that pique their

We organize books in various ways so readers can experience different approaches to choosing books. Much of our library is organized in baskets by author, topic, series, and genre. Baskets make it easy to preview front-facing books, but we have books organized spine out in case a student just wants to browse freely without knowing exactly what they are looking for.

interest. Classroom library design should answer these questions for our new students:

- What counts as reading in this classroom?
- What does it mean to be a reader in this classroom?
- Is there a place for me here?
- Do I see myself represented in the books on display?
- Do I see characters that I know?
- Do I see books I've never seen before that look interesting?
- Which types of books are valued/not valued in this classroom?
- Do I see topics that I am interested in learning more about?

These are just some of the questions we keep in mind as teachers. When we keep these questions in our mind, we listen and learn more from our students. We listen to discover the messages they get from the classroom, school, and society about what "counts" as reading. Franki had several fifth graders who kept up on sports statistics daily and always talked about them. When Franki asked why they didn't read these sites during Reading Workshop, the group looked confused. "Are we allowed to?" they asked. Franki worked with them to create a page that bookmarked the sports sites they relied on for daily reading.

Our libraries are not housed in a single area of the classroom. Instead, there are different sections of the library throughout the room. Years ago, Franki began separating the fiction and nonfiction sections of the library so students could think about their purposes for reading when choosing books. So, if they wanted to learn information, they could go to the nonfiction section. This was the first time Franki had books in more than one place in the classroom, and it changed the ways we think about the classroom library as a space.

We design the classroom library early in the year, knowing it will evolve and change throughout as students take more ownership of what they read. The original arrangement of books at the beginning of the year allows for change as readers develop their own ideas about library design. We have the opportunity in our classroom library curation and design to create a space for every reader and to use that design to support growth across the year.

In this photo of Lynsey's third-grade classroom, you can see bookshelves spread throughout the room.

Classroom library and book displays are spread throughout the room, so books can be used as reading and writing tools.

A basket of books about birds was created one year by a group of fifth graders who became interested in birds and bird watching. The basket included both fiction and nonfiction titles in a variety of formats. Baskets like this build on readers' topical interests and invite them to stretch in the types of books (e.g., genre, format, etc.) they read.

We make sure that a variety of books are on display so readers don't get the impression that only one kind of reading is valued.

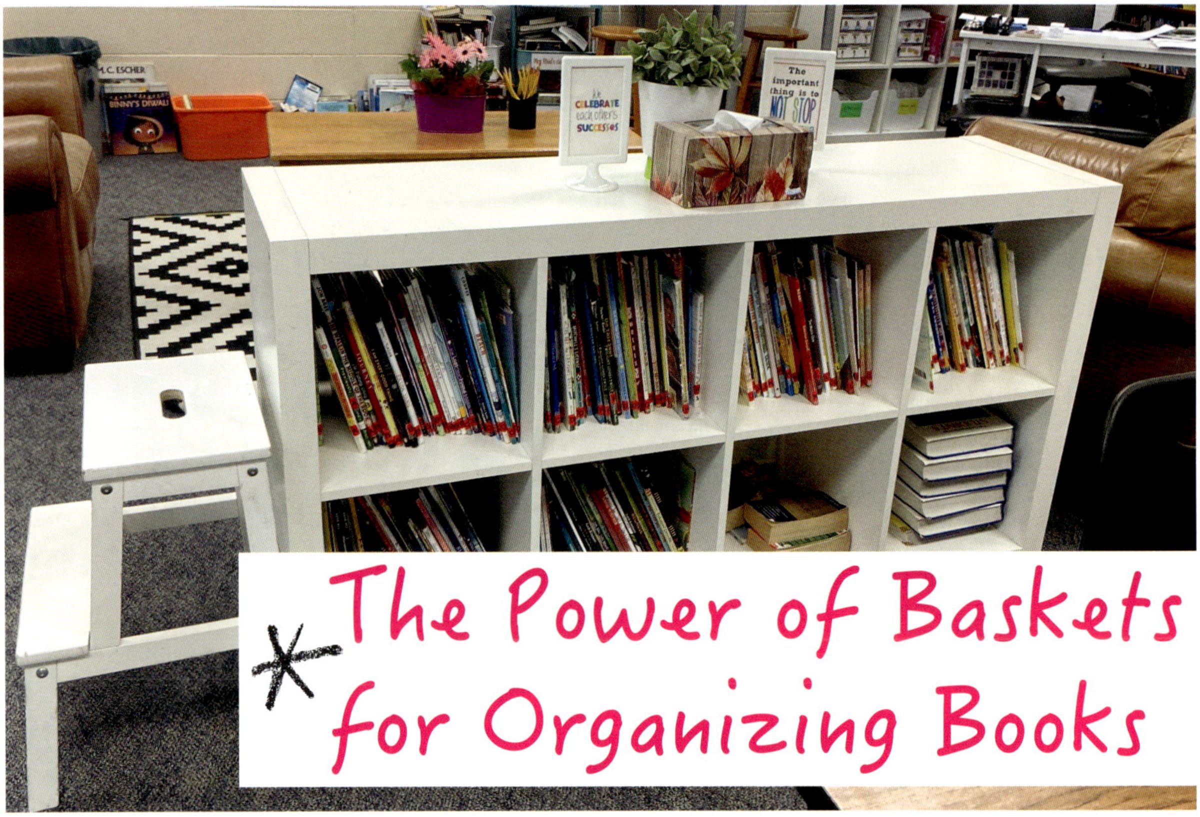

The Power of Baskets for Organizing Books

We don't have all books organized in baskets, as we believe that browsing is important. In this fourth-grade classroom, this part of the picture book collection is kept spine out and labeled and organized by author for easy browsing.

We cannot begin to imagine the number of plastic baskets and plastic bins we have purchased over the years. We love to have a large portion of the classroom library organized into book baskets. No matter the students' age, we have organized most of our books into baskets, as we have found this to be an incredible tool for supporting growing readers.

Baskets serve as a scaffold to our students as they grow as readers. One goal is for readers to be able to find their next read. But organizing our classroom libraries into baskets does so much more than that. Organizing into baskets:

- invites readers to browse face-out books;
- helps limit the overwhelming selection of books for young readers;
- supports student independence;
- supports students in thinking about their tastes and needs as readers;
- helps readers understand the categorizations of books (e.g., authors, genres, characters, format); and
- helps readers discover new books and categories.

Many teachers organize books into baskets as a management tool. But our baskets are more about supporting students as they build identities as readers than about managing our collections. We don't typically label the books within the baskets for several reasons. One big reason is that we see baskets as a thinking tool. We've seen kindergarten students place *The Very Impatient Caterpillar* by Ross Burach into the Eric Carle author basket. We've seen fifth graders who were committed to only reading books in the Diary of a Wimpy Kid series discover and fall in love with *The 13th Story Treehouse* in a nearby basket. We've seen readers go to the basket of "Quick Reads" after finishing a very long, complex book, knowing that they need a breather before the next long, complex book.

Whether we've taught kindergarten or fifth grade, we've found that children are pretty good at returning books to the right place if they understand the reasons for which readers choose different books. We've also found that there are many books that fit into multiple baskets. A book like *Everybody in the Red Brick Building* can be placed in the "Oge Mora" illustrator basket, the "Cumulative Tales" basket, or the "Books We've Read Together" basket. We are always delighted when a child puts a book in a basket/category that we haven't thought of. Or even better, we love when a child says something like "We need a basket for books that have sounds in them!" after reading a book like *Everybody in the Red Brick Building.*

Labeling books for management purposes sends the message that each book belongs in a single or correct category and that readers will choose a book for one reason alone. Instead, we want students to understand that reader identity is complex and ever-changing. One reader might choose to read *A Rover's Story* by Jasmine Warga because they love robots

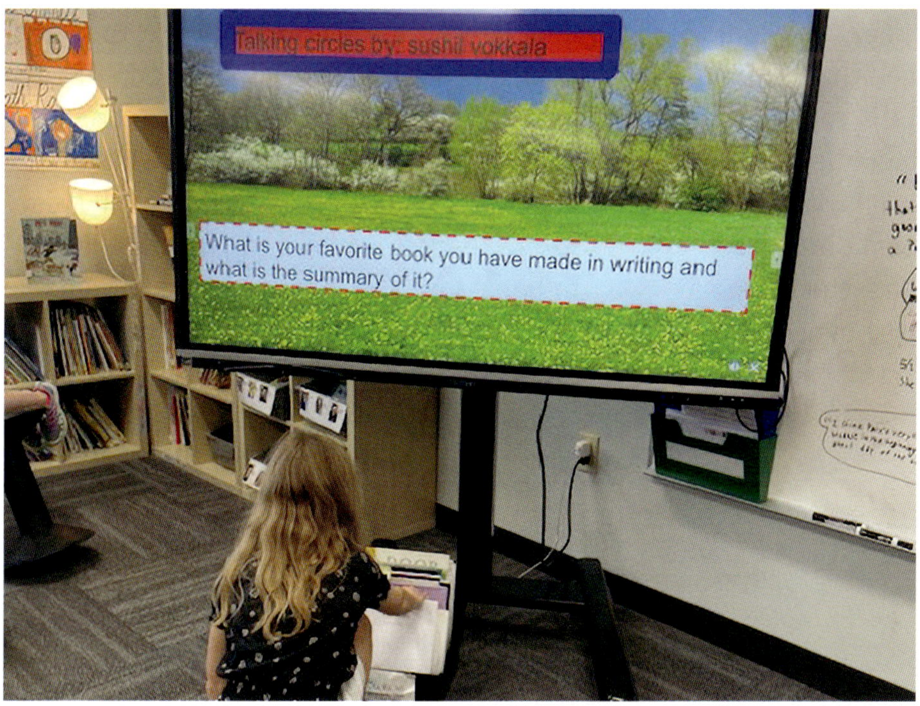

Lynsey's third graders created a basket of books for the class titled "Books We Should Read Together." Students add books to the basket when they find one that fits. This student is adding a book to that basket.

while another may choose it because they read *Other Words for Home* and fell in love with the author. We want to leave as much thinking to the reader as possible, and we want the baskets to serve as scaffolds rather than collection management tools.

When we do choose to label books, it is often for the books that are not housed in baskets. For these books, our goal is for students to name what they are reading and to think about that aspect of their choices. So, some years, we have a section of books labeled biographies or one labeled graphic novels, and those typically are created when our students are gravitating toward those books and are thinking about the kinds of reading within that genre or format that engage them.

Readers often begin the school year carrying along all they've learned from past experiences with the classroom library. Some have been taught to rely on book levels while others have not been successful at finding books they enjoy. Still others have learned that reading "fat chapter books" is what is valued. It takes weeks and weeks to build understanding together as students are invited to explore and revise the classroom library. During those first few weeks of school, we pay close attention and have many conversations about how our readers choose books, and then we build on that. We make time for students to share the reasons they choose certain books, and we might then create new baskets or rearrange shelves based on their sharing. When readers understand the library organization, the library evolves because they create baskets based on need.

One year, a fifth grader realized that he loved historical fiction written in verse. He wondered why there was no basket for books that fit those categories. Creating a basket together with Franki helped them both think about this type of book, find books that fit the category, and visit the school library to find more. This gave other classmates a new way to think about books. Some who liked historical fiction might try a verse novel; those who loved verse novels might try historical fiction.

We do commit to having some books in our classroom library that are not organized into baskets. We know that readers don't always have a plan for what to read next, and it takes some book shopping to find the perfect fit. We want our readers to be able to experience browsing without a plan and to find a book they aren't looking for. As readers, we love to visit the library or bookstore and look around until something catches our eye. We want that for all readers.

Students choose books from various baskets to support their reading and writing needs.

In Franki's fifth-grade classroom, a small group of students put this basket together, gathering all of the books that were helping them grow as writers.

The Concept of Reading Ladders and How Libraries Support Them

The goal of reading ladders is to slowly move students from where they are to where we would like them to be. With reading ladders, you start with the authors, genres, or subjects your readers like then connect them to book after book — each a little more complex or challenging than the last.

— Teri Lesesne, *Reading Ladders*, 2010

We know the important role we play as teachers to build on where students are as readers and to expand their experiences, so we take what we have learned from Dr. Lesesne to our classroom library design. We know that laddering a student's reading and suggesting they try something new is always an invitation. As our understanding of reading ladders has evolved, we have realized that good classroom library design provides a way for readers to begin to take risks and to expand their reading lives on their own. Although we love sharing books with our students, we don't want students to always rely only on us for book recommendations. Classroom library design should invite students to move from where they are to their next place as readers.

Often, children go to a bookshelf because they have fallen in love with a series. But when there are other series at their disposal to explore that are similar in some way but different in others, the library invites students to give something new a try. So, we are intentional about the baskets we put next to each other, knowing that a child may go to one basket for one book but discover another interesting title nearby in a different basket.

In this first-grade classroom, Elephant and Piggie books are placed next to the Pigeon series. If students like one series by Mo Willems, they may want to try another.

We can ladder nonfiction titles in similar ways. We might make sure to display Melissa Stewart's *Feathers: Not Just for Flying* next to *Shells: More than a Home* near each other. Series books in nonfiction give readers the opportunity to read a format they are comfortable with while exploring a new topic. We also have baskets that combine

Lynsey is intentional about placing the I Survived series near others that have similar traits. The I Survived books offer readers history, so a student who likes that series might also like the Ranger in Time books. Putting both series in a shared basket might invite readers to stretch beyond whichever they happen to be familiar with.

We've seen baskets of books called "Funny Books" at every grade level. A basket like this can serve as a reading ladder because if kids like humor, they might be willing to try a new author, a new format, or a different type of "humor" as a reader.

both fiction and nonfiction. If a reader is interested in baseball stories, they might stretch to a biography that connects people to the history of baseball. Our goal is to help students find new books they love and to grow as readers while in our classrooms. But another goal is to help them understand their role in expanding their own reading. Every time they expand as a reader, their identity as a reader grows.

We used to think that our classroom libraries had to be organized in a single way, so if we organized some books into author baskets, all other books needed to be organized that way as well. Or if we organized by genre, every book in the library needed to be organized by genre. But we have come to realize that if we want our students to have agency and to naturally grow as readers, we should offer them multiple paths to new books.

In the next few sections, we'll share some of the ways that our classroom libraries are organized and how those strategies for organizing support readers.

Organizing by Author

Author Grace Lin writes in a variety of formats. Valuing every one of these is important.

We came to understand the power of author baskets by accident. When Franki was teaching kindergarten years ago, she wanted her young readers to understand that the author of a book was a person. This was not an easy concept for new readers to understand, so she created a few baskets of books by then-favorite authors and added photos of the authors to each. Photos of Eric Carle, Laura Numeroff, and others filled the classroom library, and children then grasped the concept of an author easily!

But more happened as Franki watched the students choose and put away books. Students began sharing what they knew about different authors with one another as they gathered around the book baskets to decide in which basket a book might belong. They began to notice certain characteristics they could expect from individual authors, and they used this understanding in choosing their next books. The author baskets became a tool that does far more than simply teach students about the authors behind the stories they love — they support students in developing identity and agency as readers. When students realize they enjoy books by a certain author, they can think about why it is that they like that author's work. They begin to notice and name the qualities that they could expect when they read books by certain authors. Discussing books in this way also builds their language to talk about books and reading in more complex ways.

We find that our readers develop connections to authors and that they change as readers when we highlight authors in the classroom library. One year in third grade, *El Deafo* became the most popular book in the classroom. Franki had a student with hearing loss; she wore hearing aids and quickly fell in love with the graphic novel. She carried the book around with her and talked about it to friends, shared her thoughts in whole-class meetings, and even wrote to the author, who replied! Other students fell in love with the book too, and many wondered what other books CeCe Bell had written. Although the classroom library had many books by CeCe Bell, they hadn't yet been gathered in a basket, so the third graders were learning the power of choosing books by author, and many wanted to read more by this author they loved. So, a basket was created to house this particular author's books.

> "Scaffolding by author baskets supports readers in thinking more about the authors they love. We have found that in all grades, if we have author baskets, students start to think about the authors they read, even if there is no basket for that specific author in the classroom library."

Author baskets also serve as a scaffold for choosing books. Often, the library collection can feel overwhelming, so having a starting place for deciding on a new book is important. Just as we often go into a bookstore or library and go right to the area of books by our favorite author, we want this for our readers as well.

Scaffolding by author baskets supports readers in thinking more about the authors they love. We have found that in all grades,

Having photos of the authors on the baskets that house their books provides a scaffold for choosing books as well as for talking about books as students grow in their identities as readers.

This Christian Robinson author/illustrator basket invites readers to read across an author's/illustrator's work.

if we have author baskets, students start to think about the authors they read, even if there is no basket for that specific author in the classroom library. Often, when a child discovers a new book they love, they ask, "Do we have any other books by this author?" This is how new author baskets sometimes get created in our classrooms.

We have also discovered the power of author baskets to help children unlearn society's messages about reading chapter books, being too old to read picture books, and the limits of levels. In the Grace Lin basket, we might have her fantasy novels, her series books, her transitional early chapter books, her picture books, and her board books. We are huge fans of Grace Lin's work, and we read everything she writes. So, we don't care if one of her books is too easy or is meant for younger readers. We read it and add it to our classroom library because we love her work.

For years, we only had fiction books in author baskets. But we came to realize that authentically, readers know nonfiction authors as well. It is often more difficult to identify nonfiction books by the same author, as they may have various illustrators, formats, etc., but we know that when we love an author's writing, we will read everything that author writes. This is true across genre and format.

So, although we began with author baskets focused mainly on fiction authors, our thinking has since evolved. Nonfiction authors such as Melissa Stewart and Suzi Eszterhas and poets such as Nikki Giovanni, Douglas Florian, and Janet Wong now have author baskets in our classrooms. When our students see books organized by authors, we are sending the message that we hope they find authors they love.

Author baskets let students know that often, readers have favorite authors. It teaches them that if they love a book by an author, chances are they might like other books by that same person. Most important, it lets them know that there are many incredible authors out there, and that as they evolve as readers, there will be new authors to discover.

Organizing by Genre

A fantasy shelf in Julie Rhiel's fourth-grade classroom lets readers explore the various types of fantasy, as it may be a new genre for many of them.

Our elementary readers are often still building an understanding about what makes a genre a genre. Our readers often confuse format with genre. When we ask middle-grade readers what types of books they enjoy, they often say, "chapter books." We want to make sure we use part of the classroom library to name the genres for readers so that as they browse for books and talk about books with friends, the vocabulary and conceptual understanding around genre grows.

Readers often prefer a certain genre. Some prefer fiction while others prefer biography. When given time to reflect, a young reader might realize they enjoy narrative fiction and narrative nonfiction. So, it actually may be the format and not a specific genre that they prefer. Knowing and understanding genre and the interplay between genre and format is an important literacy skill, and it is also a tool for building reader identity.

What we want our kindergarten students to understand about genre is very different from what we want our fifth graders to understand. When Franki taught kindergarten, she put the fiction books in one corner of the room and the nonfiction books in a separate area so young readers would begin to understand the differences among the types of books they could choose to read. Her goal was for these young readers to begin to understand the concept of genre by understanding fiction versus nonfiction. Determining which section of the library to visit based on what they were looking for taught children the power in their own informed decision-making as well as a bit about genre.

But there is much more to understand about genre as children grow in age and as readers. And the field of children's literature has expanded, so there are now books that don't easily fit into just one genre.

Sometimes, our role as teachers is to help our readers name the qualities they notice about themselves when it comes to genre. If a fifth grader is enjoying the book *The War that Saved My Life*, it might be our role to point out that this is a new genre for them and to name it as historical fiction. We can let them know there is a whole shelf of other similar books that they might want to check out. When a child enjoys a new kind of book, their identity as a reader grows and changes, and their strategies for choosing books evolves.

> "When we organize by genre, those readers who discover they enjoy a certain genre have a place to begin when choosing their next book. But that isn't the only benefit of organizing by genre. When students read several books of a single genre, they begin to learn what to expect from that genre."

When we organize by genre, those readers who discover they enjoy a certain genre have a place to begin when choosing their next book. But that isn't the only benefit of organizing by genre. When students read several books of a single genre, they begin to learn what to expect from that genre. They begin to understand that if they want a book with magic, they'll look for a fantasy title, and if they read a fairy tale, they can expect a happily ever after. As readers grow through the elementary years, understanding characteristics of a specific genre often come from reading many books in that genre. Knowing genres also helps readers build literary vocabulary. As readers talk about different genres of books, the words they use grow over time, naturally building a literary vocabulary. As they start to talk about why they like a particular book or what type of book they are looking for as their next read, words specific to genre become more sophisticated.

Vocabulary around subgenres also builds agency as readers better understand the specifics of their reading tastes. For example, when a child realizes during a reading conference, "I like fantasy, but only the kind where it is like real life, not like when animals talk," it helps them choose new books and realize what makes a genre "fantasy."

A reader who likes *Wings of Fire* is a different type of fantasy reader than one who enjoys *Sal and Gabi Break the Universe*, and when a library is organized by genre, we've found that readers naturally begin to distinguish between various types of fantasy, and they might expand their tastes and discover similarities between the two. Similarly, readers who love biographies may stick with the genre but expand the topics within the genre they enjoy.

Organizing by genre in some capacity gives readers another way to think about their reading and to build strategies for taking ownership of their reading lives.

When students can browse a variety of books within a genre, such as biographies, they begin to think more deeply about their tastes as readers. They also might find books that invite them to expand the types of books they typically read.

Within the genre of biography, Katie Papesh's fourth graders realized they had certain topics within the genre that they each preferred. So, they created subcategories for the many picture book biographies in the classroom library.

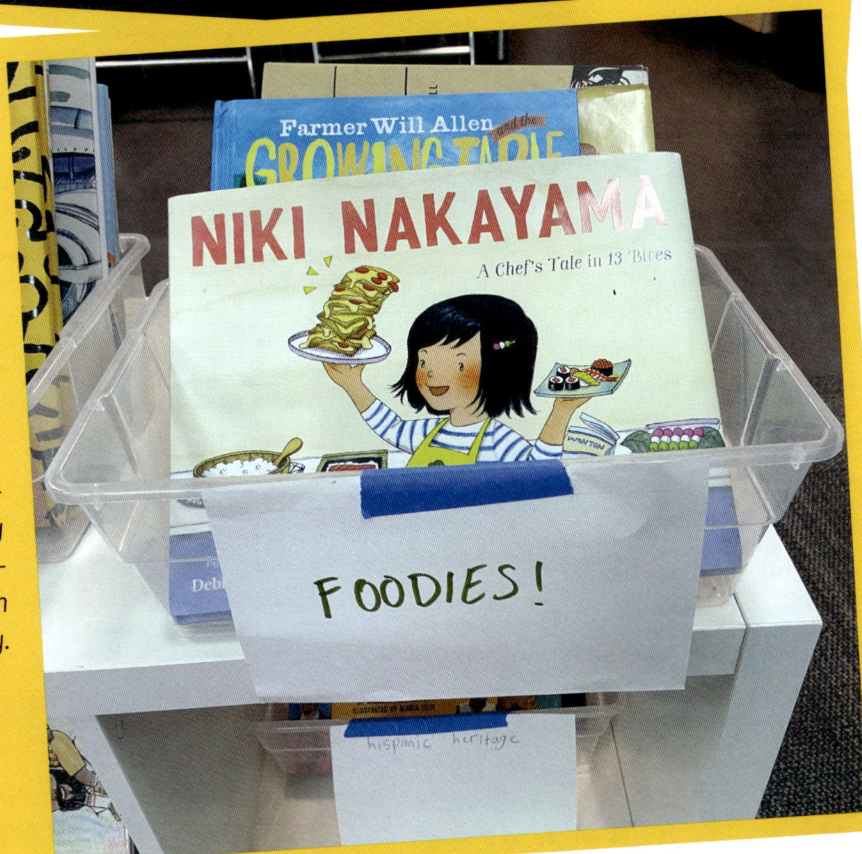

Organizing by Series

These series books are part of Lynsey's third-grade classroom.

Most readers can name a childhood series that hooked them. For Franki, it was the Nancy Drew series. Memories of choosing a new Nancy Drew book each Sunday from the shelf in her grandma's attic are some of her favorites. Nancy Drew books were key to Franki's growth and identity as a reader. Decades later, she can still picture Nancy's house, her car, and details from some of Franki's favorite mysteries.

Readers of all ages read series books and it is often in elementary grades that readers first discover the joy of reading about characters they love. We also know when a child reads another book in a favorite series, they come to the book with different expectations that support understanding. No matter the age we've taught, we've seen the power of series books on our readers, whether they fall in love with *Don't Let the Pigeon Drive the Bus!* and are excited to read any other book that Mo Willems writes about the Pigeon, or whether they get hooked on the Crossover series by Kwame Alexander.

We have seen repeatedly in our classrooms how a series can change the trajectory of a reader's journey and how students tend to read with more depth when they are hooked on a series. We don't worry when a child spends a good part of a school year reading the same series; we know that being hooked on a series is an important phase in many readers' development.

When we organize books by series, we support readers in finding books, but we also help them begin to understand that many readers enjoy books in a series. Organizing books by series can invite conversations around the specifics of a series. Is it the character that draws us to the series? Is it the genre?

After discovering Nancy Drew, Franki realized that she loved mysteries, so she spent a good deal of her upper elementary years reading as many mystery series as she could find. Falling in love with a series can help you realize what it is that engages you as a reader and what keeps you reading more. And, it is a launching point for many young readers.

We can't count the number of readers who have started the year stating they only read Captain Underpants and Diary of a Wimpy Kid, and they are waiting until the next book in the series is released to dive back in. Many of these children come to our classrooms not seeing themselves as readers, yet they have discovered a series they love. Building on this love is the next step. We know that falling in love with these series will help them fall in love with other series like Dragons in a Bag, Marya Khan, and Desmond Cole Ghost Patrol.

Series are powerful for readers at all ages. A student whose first language was French recalled a mystery series she had read a year earlier that she loved and was hoping to reread in English. She asked Franki about the series, and together they got online, searching to see if the series was available in English. They found three books in the series to add to the classroom library. Once the student reread and shared them, other classmates enjoyed the books, and they were able to recommend other mystery series that were similar.

We used to wait until we had the whole series to create a basket, but we've come to realize that it doesn't matter how many books in a series we have; the important thing is that readers know they can find more books in a series they love in a specific basket or at the library.

Books organized by series or author on the shelf in Franki's fifth-grade classroom.

This is a series book basket in a first-grade classroom.

Organizing by Format

We used to have three areas of the classroom library: picture books, chapter books, and poetry books. We organized the books that way mostly for our own organizational and management purposes — it was easier to manage the space and to find the books we were looking for. But since that time, we have become less worried about managing the classroom library and more interested in making sure it serves as a third teacher in the classroom. Student needs and student growth are the keys to our organizational decision-making.

We have learned so much from our students since the years when we used to organize our classroom libraries that way. And books have evolved so much that there are many new formats, including hybrid ones. Organizing part of the library by format helps us to extend what readers will read. It is a great way to support readers in their growth. When young readers are committed to a certain format, they are willing to try other books in that same format. Because of this, picture books, magazines, graphic novels, poetry, ebooks, and audiobooks are also important formats to highlight in our classrooms.

When students choose books by format, we want there to be opportunities within the format to help them evolve as readers. If a student loves graphic novels, we want to build on that. It is possible to read graphic novels in all genres, so if we highlight the graphic novel format itself and then organize by genre within that, our graphic novel readers may be confident enough to try a new genre within a format they already love.

Having many of the graphic novels in one section of the room supports readers in guiding them to books in that format while also perhaps inviting them to try a new series, author, or genre within the format.

We have found the same to be true for verse novels. Students who read Kwame Alexander's *The Crossover* are likely to read something else in the verse format. This book changed many students' perceptions of reading, as they were more engaged due to the format. Readers who loved *The Crossover* might not think they like science fiction, but when they see that *Alone* by Megan E. Freeman is set up in a similar format, they may decide to give it a try and maybe find that they like it.

By including format sections of the classroom library, such as a shelf of verse novels or a shelf of graphic novels, we can invite our young readers to choose and grow based on a format they are most comfortable reading, and make it easy for them to identify new formats they would like to explore.

Poetry comes into play when we think about organizing by format. How might we sub-organize poetry into types of poetry (e.g., haiku) or topics of poetry (birds, for instance) or genres of poetry (biography)? We tend to have a poetry section and include poetry in many other areas of the classroom library as well.

What Counts?

It is also helpful for us to think about format areas of the library because it keeps us, as teachers, accountable for knowing what we count as reading. Further, it helps our students understand that all formats count as reading and that no one format is better than another. We worry when teachers don't count graphic novels or picture books as reading, and by making sure these and other formats are visible and displayed intentionally, we're sending the message that any and all reading is valued.

Displaying several poetry books invites readers to try a new format and to explore a new-to-them section of the classroom library.

Organizing Graphic Novels

There are various ways to organize graphic novels depending on our readers. Sometimes we have a section designated to graphic novels and other times we have graphic novels embedded into other areas of the classroom library.

Just as the publication of graphic novels for children has evolved, so has our thinking about that format in our classroom libraries. Early on, when few graphic novels for young readers were being published, we housed the few that were appropriate for middle-grade readers in a basket. We soon added a few great series, such as Babymouse and Lunch Lady, and we then had baskets of graphic novels categorized by series. Eventually, the graphic novels in our classrooms took up an entire tall bookshelf of their own.

It was about that time when we realized that graphic novels were a format, and that although many readers choose books by format, many others do not. We also knew that some of our students were choosing to exclusively read graphic novels while others avoided them. We knew that the way we had organized and displayed these books could serve as invitations for both groups of readers.

As our graphic novel collections continued to grow, separating them out sent a message that graphic novels were all the same and that they were simultaneously different from other books in the classroom.

We want our readers to know that every format of text (e.g., graphic novels, poetry, blog posts, etc.) counts. Sometimes, separating a format out helps support readers in expanding the formats they read. But sometimes, separating them limits readers. So, we must look at the readers in front of us to see how to use the setup to invite growth.

"We want our readers to know that every format of text (i.e., graphic novels, poetry, blog posts, etc.) counts. Sometimes, separating a format out helps support readers in expanding the formats they read. But sometimes, separating them limits readers. So, we must look at the readers in front of us to see how to use the setup to invite growth."

Currently, graphic novels have been embedded in the rest of the classroom library because even though many readers choose graphic novels for the format, we wanted our readers to know that they could read graphic novels across different genres. And we wanted them to think about the ways in which graphic novels were different and to ask themselves whether they liked the format or if they were drawn to a certain genre of graphic novel. So now, you might find *Hoops* by Matt Tavares in the sports basket in the nonfiction area of the library. Readers looking for a graphic novel might stretch their reading to the topic of sports, even if it's entirely new to them. Meanwhile, readers interested in sports might realize they enjoy a graphic novel now and then.

When we studied bookstore and library designs, we learned that good organization of books gives readers various entry points. A romance book might be in the romance section display, and a copy of the same title might be shelved with the author's other titles. Yet another copy might live on the Staff Picks shelf. Bookstores and libraries know that readers choose books for a variety of reasons and that the way books are displayed often invites those seeing them to stretch a bit as readers. We tend to do this with graphic novels when we have more than one copy. Instead of housing them together, we may put them in different areas of the library. For example, *Mighty Jack* by Ben Hatke might be housed in the Ben Hatke author basket and also in the "Fairy Tales" basket.

With graphic novels, we can do several different things, depending on our goals for readers. If we had unlimited funds for books, we would have a few copies of popular titles and put one in the graphic novel area, one in the author basket and, one on the new books display. But since we typically only have a single copy of a book, we must decide, and there is really no wrong decision . . . and no permanent decision.

Organizing New Books

Readers always find new books displayed in several areas of the classroom.

There is nothing like discovering a new book that you fall in love with. Franki recently browsed the "New Books" section of her local bookstore, where Lisa See's *Lady Tan's Circle of Women* caught her eye. She bought the book, fell in love with it, passed it on to a friend, and then looked for other books by author Lisa See.

There is a reason bookstores and libraries have a display called "New Books" at the entrance. Readers love new books and the idea of discovering a new gem. Many readers (Franki included) love to read books that are "hot off the press" or that are on the current bestseller lists. Franki also likes to know when a favorite author is releasing a new book so she can get it right away.

Of course, we don't always read only new books, but keeping up with new books is something many readers do. When we build displays and conversations around new books into our classroom library design, it gives children messages as readers.

It helps them think about their own reading in new ways and continues to help them build their identity and agency as readers.

Paying attention to new and upcoming book releases supports readers' growth in a variety of ways.

- Anticipating books helps readers begin to articulate the reasons they think they'll like a certain book.
- Anticipating books means that readers are thinking ahead and planning for their future reading life.
- When readers anticipate the newest book by a beloved author or the next book in a favorite series, they have expectations based on what they already know about that author or series.
- When browsing new books that they know nothing about, readers are forced to think about whether they'd like the book and the reasons for their decision. As they think about each new book, they learn a bit more about themselves.
- Much of the information about new releases comes from word of mouth (in person or digitally). This invites conversations with others who might like the same types of books. Talking to other readers is a huge part of growing as a reader.
- Anticipating new books often leads readers to reviewers they can trust. Sharing sources like *The Horn Book Magazine* and the blog American Indians in Children's Literature allows readers to see that there are expert sources for new books.

Organizing Nonfiction

Rethinking Design of the Nonfiction Collection in the Classroom Library

Young people need adults who foster access to high-quality nonfiction books because they appreciate the power of these titles to excite and inspire as well as inform readers of all ages.

— NCTE Position Statement on the Role of Nonfiction Literature (K–12) (2023)

We must take the same care in organizing the nonfiction sections of our classroom libraries as we do when organizing the other sections. NCTE's *Position Statement on the Role of Nonfiction Literature (K–12)* reminds us that "too often, students are not given the time and freedom to explore topics of personal interest or enthusiastically share their new knowledge with others." It is easy as teachers to focus on the fiction section of our library and then put the nonfiction in another section.

A book display about the environment might include a variety of genres.

However, this sends the wrong message to our students.

Until recently, we organized nonfiction into topics. We tended to add to our classroom libraries nonfiction books that connected in some way to the science and social studies units we were required to teach. So, we might have had baskets of outer space books and some baskets of books about rocks. Sometimes, we'd separate out biographies within the nonfiction section. But our nonfiction books were not curated with the goal of independent reading, and they were not organized in a way that engaged or grew readers.

We've watched our students and we've read and studied the nonfiction books for children that have been published in the last decade. In doing so, we've found new and better ways to organize parts of our nonfiction collection in order to invite reading and growth. We realized we did not put the same amount of time and energy into getting to know nonfiction authors, series, and new releases as we did with fiction. So, years ago, we committed to reading and knowing more nonfiction titles that might be engaging for our students.

Because of that commitment, we have discovered that authors and series are not only important for readers of fiction. In fact, Franki became obsessed with the Scientist in the Field series one year after reading *The Hive Detectives: Chronicles of a Honeybee Catastrophe* by Loree Griffin Burns. Because of her love of this book, she looked for more books in the series and was willing to read about new topics. She also discovered other books by Griffin Burns, and realized she loved her as an author. Franki also read a bit more about honeybees. This one book changed her as a nonfiction reader as she discovered a series, an author, and a topic that all engaged her as a reader.

We still organize some books by topic, but we don't choose books based on required units of study in the content areas anymore. Instead, we look for books that address topics of interest to elementary students. We've reorganized so that we also have baskets of nonfiction series and authors. We have found that when students discover nonfiction authors or series

Nonfiction Author Baskets

Loree Griffin Burns
Jason Chin
Suzi Eszterhas
Jess Keating
Kadir Nelson
Shelley Rotner
Duncan Tonatiuh
Carole Boston Weatherford
Seymour Simon
Melissa Stewart

Nonfiction Series Baskets

Scientists in the Field
The World of Weird Animals
Block Board Books
Hidden Animals
Busy Baby Animals
Science Comics
History Smashers
Who Would Win?
Everything Awesome About
Over and Under
The Truth About

When nonfiction is curated and organized intentionally, students read and share nonfiction joyfully during independent reading time.

New informational books are displayed in bins in Lynsey's classroom.

they love, just as with fiction, they may read through the entire collection.

We also create categories of nonfiction within our libraries as we get to know our readers each year, and we think about those students and how they choose nonfiction books. We listen as they share the books they are reading and the reasons they are enjoying them. Reading conferences often give us some insights into these topics, and we can help them name the types of books they are discovering. Some baskets we've created in the past after listening to students include:

- Books You Can Read in Any Order
- Funny Nonfiction
- How-To Books
- Fact Books
- Anthologies
- Books with Interesting Visuals

We've also thought about reading ladders when it comes to nonfiction, so we create baskets such as a Bird Books, which includes biography, field guides, fact books, and more. For readers who are interested in birds, this invites them to stick with the topic but to try new formats and subgenres.

Once we started to pay as much attention to our nonfiction collection as we did

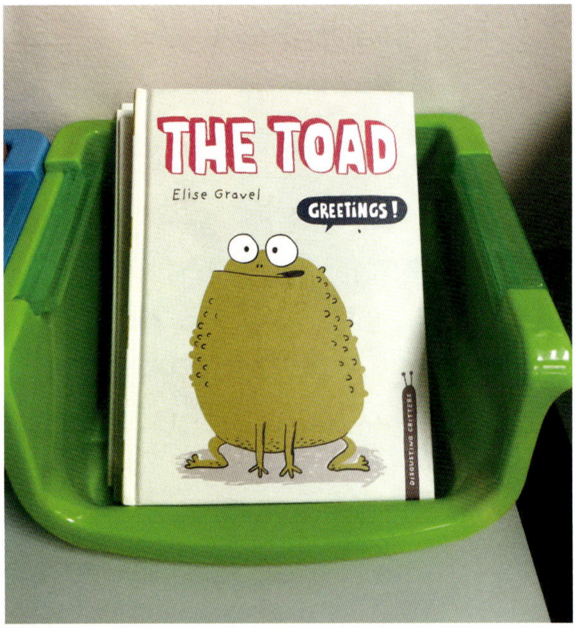

When we put nonfiction series books together, readers often extend their reading to read a topic they may not have otherwise been interested in.

to the rest of our classroom library, more readers began choosing nonfiction works for independent reading time. They discovered favorite nonfiction authors and series they enjoyed. It is easy to fall into traditional patterns when curating and organizing our nonfiction section of the library, but if we want to engage readers in nonfiction, we must push back on those traditional ways of organizing and design this section of the library with the same care and intentionality that we use for the fiction collection.

Some readers just want to browse nonfiction to see what catches their attention. We want some sections of our library to invite that kind of browsing.

A Note on Biographies

Young readers love stories about people, so our nonfiction collections often have a biography section where students can find books about incredible people. We want to note that we are careful about biography series that have a single author. We are committed to finding books by authors who know and understand the stories they are telling, so we tend to rely more on individual biographies than series.

Finding spaces to display nonfiction series books, magazines, etc., helps readers discover new books.

A basket of nonfiction books that support writers is displayed on top of a shelf in the classroom.

"If You Liked. . ." Baskets

An "If You Liked. . ." basket in a third-grade classroom.

In our favorite bookstores and libraries, we often see displays recommending books based on a book we've already read and loved. These "If You Liked. . ." displays help us find books that we think we might fall in love with because we fell in love with one that was similar in some way.

When we create these "If You Liked. . ." collections or baskets, we are hoping to introduce our readers to books they may not otherwise discover, and we are also hoping they begin to learn a bit more about themselves as readers as they begin to define for themselves what it is they enjoyed about a certain book. When we invite students to consider both subjects, they begin to build new strategies for choosing their next reads.

Recently, *Odder* by Katherine Applegate was a popular read. This verse novel about a young otter is a fictional account that was inspired by the true story of the Monterey Bay Aquarium. When a book is popular and being read by many in our classroom community, we like to create an invitational "If You Liked. . ." basket. Sometimes, we do this on our own, sometimes we do this alongside students, and sometimes students create these on their own.

In the "If You Liked *Odder*" basket, we included the following books for the following reasons. Each book was included to give readers a way to think about exactly what they loved about the book *Odder*. Each recommendation was meant to give students something comfortable that they'd experienced as a reader as well as something new they might find they enjoy.

There is no right or wrong way to create these "If You Liked. . ." baskets. Instead, we rely on our understanding of the ways in which our students are getting to know themselves as readers and try to build on that in some way. The power of these baskets is in giving readers an invitation to think more deeply about the reasons they liked a book and to begin to expand the types of books they realize engage them.

Books in the "If You Liked Odder" Basket and Why They Fit

Books	Why You Might Like It
Wishtree by Katherine Applegate	It is by the same author but a very different type of book.
Other Words for Home by Jasmine Warga	It is a novel in verse, which is the same format as *Odder.*
The Aquanaut: A Graphic Novel by Dan Santat	It is a graphic novel connected to the sea but is also science fiction, which is a different genre.
The Secret Life of the Sea Otter by Laurence Pringle	It is a nonfiction book for readers who might want to know more about sea otters.
The World's Loneliest Elephant by Ralph Fletcher	It is a book about an animal rescue, and *Odder* may have piqued students' curiosity about this kind of work.

Displaying Books in the Classroom

Katrina Webber displays books outside her classroom each month as an invitation to the school community to get to know new books and new authors. These books were displayed in November as part of Native American Heritage Month.

Years ago, in the middle of winter, when Franki was an elementary school librarian, a kindergarten student came into the library, scanned the bookshelves, became frustrated, and demanded, "I need a book about FLOWERS and SUN!" Franki chuckled, as she too could have used some flowers and sun on this cold and gray day. She also realized that it wasn't easy for this child to find a book about flowers, as most of the books on display were set in winter. No wonder the child was frustrated.

This student helped push Franki's thinking about her display choices. Traditionally, libraries, schools, and classrooms highlight books that go along with a time of year. For example, in October, we see books about apples, fall, and pumpkins everywhere. However, readers do not typically choose books based on seasons or upcoming holidays. Instead, they find topics, authors, and genres they enjoy. So, when a child walks into a classroom or library and the books displayed are focused on a season or a celebration, it can become difficult for them to find their next read.

Additionally, when books are displayed in this way, the displays are often lacking in books in which children can see themselves represented or that celebrate a variety of voices. We want to be thoughtful about our book displays across the year and be responsive to our students as readers. We want to use our displays as invitations to children to grow as readers, not as seasonal decorations.

As Donalyn Miller and Colby Sharp remind us in *Game Changer! Book Access for ALL Kids* (2018):

> When children cannot see themselves or their families represented in the

books we offer, we communicate that their stories don't matter, or worse, warrant shame. The lack of relevant, positive, affirming books for every child often perpetuates stereotypes, children's self-perception of otherness and institutional and social constructs that marginalize and oppress many people.

Let's think about the purpose of our displays. When we display books, we are amplifying them and giving them our stamp of approval. If we are designing classroom libraries for student agency, then our displays serve as a scaffold for readers as they grow and change and become increasingly independent. What our students see in these displays matters.

Changing displays often is important, but understanding the power of these displays and the ways that displays amplify books is critical, too. When we know that most readers choose books based on authors, genres, mood, etc., we can begin to create displays across the year that amplify authors of diverse backgrounds, based on how students will be likely to browse.

We also want to make sure we are not only amplifying books that are "grade-level text." As readers, we consume books of varying reading levels, and we don't want to give readers the message that it is not okay to read a book that is too easy, too short, or too simple.

Although we've both moved away from seasonal displays, we are intentional about our displays during heritage months. While we don't want to display books by Asian American authors only during Asian American and Pacific Islander Heritage Month, we do not want to ignore important months in our displays either. We like to use these months to highlight and celebrate authors and to get to know new books and authors to then read throughout the year.

Katrina Webber is the English language teacher at Lynsey's school. Each month, she adorns the table in front of her classroom with books representing the lived experiences of communities celebrated in corresponding history/celebration months. Lynsey watches as teachers and students stop by to pick up the books, look through

Rather than have all the books displayed together in one location, we have books displayed in several areas of the classroom. We have found that having a few books here and there invites readers to pay attention in different ways—to stop and look.

There are so many ways to display books. In this kindergarten classroom, books are displayed on some of the tables, and these are changed out frequently, sometimes by the teacher, sometimes by students.

them, ask to borrow one or two, and even smile when a book reminds them of themselves. This monthly tradition of displaying books has become important to the students and teachers in Lynsey's school. Lynsey has even been able to use the tradition Katrina started to support her own learning of new books.

Many teachers ask us how we incorporate more representational literature into our classroom libraries and curricula. This is a great way to start. During the celebration months of communities of marginalized people, take the time to read the picture books on all the displays and lists you see on Instagram, Twitter, Facebook, or at your local library.

We appreciate Katrina's displays because, in her classroom, these books are displayed all year long. She does not only display them during the celebration month; instead, she takes the opportunity to highlight these for the broader school community as an invitation to get to know these works and authors and add them to their reading lives.

As Lynsey and her students pass by Katrina's room and discover new books and authors, Lynsey thinks about ways some of those books could fit into her own curriculum. For example, in her class's Writing Workshop, Lynsey traditionally reads Marla Frazee's book *Rollercoaster* to show a moment in time, but after reading and studying books during these celebration/history months, she now uses:

- *Saturday* by Oge Mora
- *Dumplings for Lily* by Melissa Iwai
- *Pride Puppy!* by Robin Stevenson
- *I See You See* by Richard Jackson and Patrice Barton
- *Powwow Day* by Traci Sorell

Lynsey's students often borrow a book from Katrina's display and suggest adding it to their classroom library. Students and teachers discover authors and then build on those discoveries.

Regularly changing the books that are displayed keeps our libraries fresh and our readers engaged in discovering new books (as well as new qualities about themselves as readers). But these displays must be focused on authentic ways in which readers choose books. They must be designed to scaffold independence and to support every growing reader.

Students are instrumental in keeping these displays fresh. Early in the year, we may suggest students add a book to a display following a reading conference. Or we might invite a group of children who enjoy the same series to display the books in that series basket on a shelf or a book ledge. Students quickly pick up on the role of book displays as a way to amplify books, and so they become intentional and purposeful about revising displays naturally as needed.

We want to alert students that they will notice new books throughout the room all year long. Often, our displays focus on new books we've added to the classroom library. Sometimes, specific books are being displayed because of something we've noticed about our readers. Other times, we display a format or books by an author that readers have not engaged with recently.

We also use displays to place value on a variety of books. We display books of all genres, formats, and levels of difficulty so readers get the message that all reading is valued. We are proponents of picture books and board books at all grade levels, so you'll always see those on display in our classrooms. We also highlight books and authors that represent the global majority.

Book displays invite conversations between readers. We often notice a

TIP: Make Refreshing Displays a Regular Part of Classroom Library Maintenance

Changing displays is something that is a quick part of our weekly routine. Typically, much of the work of changing displays involves filling in holes as readers pull books to read from the displays. As they take books from a display to add to their own book bins, we want to fill that spot. This is the easiest way to keep books rotating. We also keep an eye out for displayed books that haven't received much attention. There is no reason for those books to take up prime display space. And when new books arrive from a book order, we often add those to the displays. So, when we change displays, we are looking to:

- fill all display space;
- remove books that haven't been picked up from the display for a while;
- add books by an author or from a series that children have just discovered;
- display books similar to others that are popular in the classroom;
- ensure displays have diverse representation, including diverse authors, characters, and genres;
- include new-to-the-classroom books; and
- make sure to always display books of varied reading levels and lengths.

group gathering having a conversation about one or more of the books when we change out those books on display in an area of the classroom.

Beyond helping students find their next books, keeping book displays fresh can be a way to:

- invite readers to try something new as they grow and change;
- remind readers of old favorites or new books in a favorite series;
- support book-selection strategies;
- introduce a genre or format that might be new to readers;
- illustrate how books might go together;
- highlight new authors; or
- introduce new characters.

Amplifying the Digital Texts

It is hard to "display" ebooks, blog posts, or audiobooks. But when we do not amplify this type of reading, we give our readers the message that these do not count as reading. Adding QR codes to books that invite readers to watch the author interview, creating a bulletin board with audiobook reviews, and posting QR codes to blogs written for children are some ways we make these texts visible as part of our classroom libraries.

Book displays can be used to help students connect conversations to past books they've read. This display from Franki's fifth-grade classroom of "Books We Read Together" is a mid-year display that continued to grow as students finished more books. These were the books Franki had read aloud to the class so far.

Taking advantage of every space to display books is something we see in many classrooms. You never know where or when a book might catch a reader's eye, so having books in various places and at various levels is important. We know that changing book displays around the room is a powerful tool.

When we display books that we've read together, we send the message that reread-ing books is valued.

We display books around the room all year long. We must be intentional about the books we amplify. We want every reader to see books they love, books they have never seen before, books that make them feel like they can find books to read here. Most important, we want to amplify books in which students see themselves.

Connecting to the School and Public Libraries

You don't need a full collection of books to create a basket. The organization is teaching readers how they choose books, and not having all the books in a series often encourages them to use the school or public libraries once they fall in love with a series.

We are often asked about whether our students use the school and public libraries, given that we have such a large collection of books in our classrooms. The definitive answer is "yes!" Not only do our students use the school and public libraries, but we set our classroom library up in a way that teaches them the importance of all libraries. Using the school and community libraries is part of what we want our readers to learn, and the ways we design our classroom libraries can support this learning.

We used to wait to create a basket of books until we had enough books to fill that basket. We only had so much space to work with, so this approach made sense. But we came to realize that it wasn't the quantity of books in the basket that matters; instead, the baskets gave readers a way to think about book choice. So, when the Percy Jackson series was the most popular book in our classroom, we had the first couple of books in the series, and these were housed in the "Percy Jackson" series basket. When readers needed book #3 in the series, they knew Mrs. Clark, our fabulous librarian, would have it in the library. This realization changed how we decided which books were housed in a series, character, or author basket.

We realized that we could be intentional about only having a few books in a popular series, thus encouraging students to visit the school or public libraries for those we did not have. We remind ourselves that the baskets serve as a way for readers to discover books they love, not to provide every book they might ever want to read.

We also make sure to embed the library websites into our online spaces, as we want our readers to know the varied places they can access books. For a book that is not available in the classroom or school libraries, our readers know to check the Columbus Metropolitan Library site, and they know they can hold the book they're seeking by using their cards, or we can pick it up for them. Just as we get books from several places, we want students to have access and skill to use the various sources of books at their disposal. Our goal in designing the classroom library is not for them to find every book they're looking for in our classroom library, but to offer a gateway for further exploration.

When students know themselves and their preferences as readers, they can find what they are looking for in the school library.

Organizing What You Have

Mandy Robek, a third-grade teacher, spreads out all her books when she begins to reorganize them for the year ahead so that she can pull out sets of books she thinks go well together.

Every year, we organize our classroom library collections, and every year, we think we have figured it out so that we will never have to organize them again. But then we buy new books, different books become popular, our students are different, and we evolve in our thinking. So, almost every year, we've found ourselves standing in front of piles of books, overwhelmed by the task ahead. Yet we've found some steps help to make the task easier.

Now we can look at what we have with fresh eyes. We look at books that seem to fall naturally into categories. We think about our readers the past year and the ways in which they connected books. Again, we listen to our students closely at the beginning of the year – they often come in looking for a certain book or topic. Those first few weeks help us continue to organize

Strategies for Organizing and Reorganizing What You Have

- Scan the books in your collection.
- Ask yourself, which have been popular? Which have gone untouched?
- Look for patterns: books in a series, books on a topic, books by an author, etc.
- Start putting books that go together in piles.
- Scan the books again.
- Look for nontraditional patterns (e.g., Are there books on dogs in various genres that you can organize together? Are there several "books that make you laugh"?).
- Determine which books you don't need anymore.
- Notice gaps in diversity of authors, genres, format, length, and difficulty.
- Determine how you might organize any new books into the collection.
- Jot down noticeable gaps so that you have a priority to fill in when you are able.

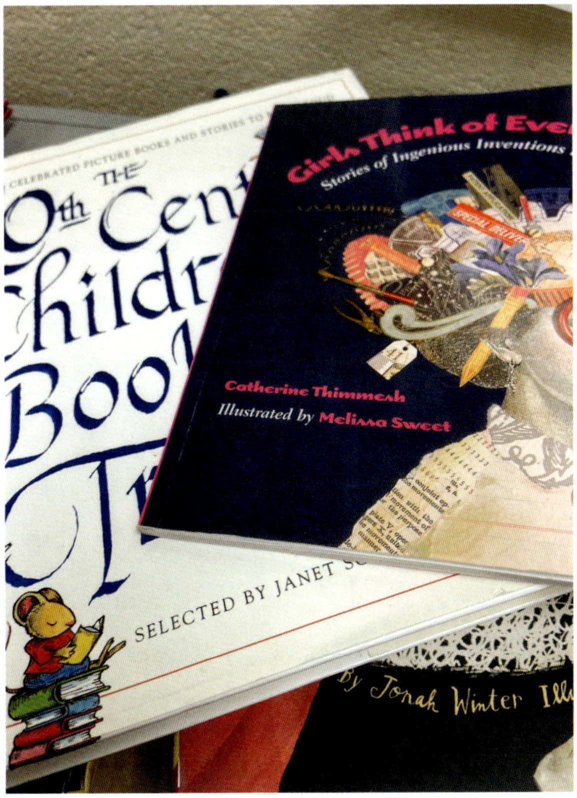

Our friend Mary Brothers, a first-grade teacher, noticed a few characters and authors that were featured in several books. She also discovered several fiction books about dogs. And there were some books that we weren't sure what to do with until we realized they were all anthologies. So, we created some author baskets, some character baskets, a "Dogs" basket and a "Collections of Stories" basket.

all that we have. One year, a student who was an expert on otters asked for otter books. There were a few random books on the subject (fiction and nonfiction) spread throughout the library, but those were quickly placed together in a topic basket. It only takes us doing this alongside students a few times early in the year for students to begin to gather sets of books that go together in some way and label those for others.

We tend to spread books out and make a big mess to begin with during this yearly reorganization process. In the past, we used to look at our collections and see all that was missing and get the urge to run out and buy lots of new books. But now, we look at what we have and find the patterns there.

It is easy to spot books in a series or several books with a favorite character. But then, we look in a more open-ended way. We might find that we have many nonfiction poetry books or a stack of wordless picture books. We may realize that we have several books that play with words or that fit into a how-to category.

We used to try to organize the entire collection in one way (e.g., by genre, alphabetical by author, etc.), but we have learned that it is best for our readers when there are many ways to "shop" for a book. So, starting with what we have and categorizing those in intentional ways is our first step.

Once we've done some general sorting, we then begin to place piles of books in the area of the room where we think they might end up. Organizing within bigger categories comes later.

Our classrooms often look like this over the summer as we sort through and create piles of books, determining the varied ways in which different ones might go together.

Sometimes, a new series only has one or two books published. When we have lots of single books in a series, we could create a basket of "New Series You Might Like."

*Auditing Our Classroom Library

We often scan the shelves of our classroom library, always reflecting and revising what we see based on what we know about our students as well as the gaps we notice in the books we curate and amplify. Auditing our classroom library is an ongoing process — no matter how careful we are to fill the gaps we see, we always find new gaps.

When we organize with author baskets, we can look at our classroom collections in an objective way. Because we put photos of the authors on many of the baskets, we can look at the people whose work we are amplifying. We can ask ourselves about the authors whose books we rely on, whose books we display, whose books we recommend. By scanning the author baskets, it is easy to see some of the gaps that need to be filled.

One day, Lynsey remembers one of her students saying, “Mrs. Burkins, I really love the Sofia Martinez series books. Are there any like that but with Indian girls?” Lynsey quickly realized that no, she didn’t have any series books in her classroom library that featured South Asian girls, and she wasn’t sure if there were any at the time. Not only was this a gap in the classroom library, but it was a gap in how Lynsey was paying attention to and searching for new books. She quickly began to think about the identities in the classroom library that needed more representation or any representation at all if they weren’t there.

We may notice that we have mostly male authors highlighted. We might notice that we have very few Latinx authors. We want to make sure that when we think about representation, we include authors who write stories that have diversity in race, gender, religion, age, sexuality, etc.

We also want to fill any gaps we have in formats. For years, we could not keep up with our young readers who were hooked on graphic novels. Once we built our graphic novel collection, we realized that within that collection, we were heavy on fantasy and realistic fiction graphic novels but had a gap when

TIP Look at Your Own Reading Gaps

It is often easier to think about the genres, authors, and characters we gravitate toward as readers, so it is helpful to know your personal gaps as a reader.

If you don’t love historical fiction, does that show up in the books you choose for your classroom library? Do you tend to add only the types of books that you enjoy? By reflecting on our own gaps as readers, we can push ourselves to read outside of our own tastes and preferences (or to read and expand our tastes and preferences!) to curate a collection that meets the needs of all readers.

it came to nonfiction graphic novels.

When we look for gaps in our classroom library, we notice diversity across:

- characters
- authors
- formats
- genres
- topics
- text difficulty levels
- lengths

It took us years to realize that as teachers, we tended to curate collections of books that we personally connected with. Or, we would pay particular attention to the books that our own children read at home and so purchased them for the classroom library. We'd also pay attention to the popular books in our classroom and build on those series and authors. But we realized that was ultimately limiting our students.

Filling Gaps in the Classroom Library

We used to build most of our nonfiction collection with books that went along with science or social studies units of study. For instance, if we knew that there was a unit on rocks and minerals, we added books that we could use to teach those concepts. But we discovered that those topics were not necessarily the books readers chose to read independently. So, we had to think very differently in order to fill the gaps in our nonfiction areas of the library that were linked to students' topics of interest.

One way we begin auditing and filling the gaps in our classroom library is by thinking about the books we share in read-aloud and mini-lessons and taking a hard look at the kinds of books we choose to amplify in our classrooms. As Dr. Mariana Souto-Manning states in an interview with *Education Week* titled "Author Interview: No More Culturally Irrelevant Teaching,"

> It is important to understand that having a handful of 'multicultural' or 'diverse' books is not enough. As Dr. Rudine Sims Bishop suggested, classrooms need to have books that serve as mirrors, windows, and sliding glass doors. Often, teachers have the idea that they have diverse books, but it is important to engage in a thorough assessment — not only of the books you have in your classroom library, that you read aloud, and that are featured in the curriculum.

So, we scan our book baskets to see if the books we amplify and highlight are those that have some gaps. (Hint: There are always gaps.)

- What are the patterns?
- What is missing in the books being shared with students?
- What's missing in the classroom library?
- Which books do I tend to booktalk and share with students? Which books do students booktalk and share?
- How inclusive are the books I choose for read-alouds and mini-lesson work as well as across content areas?
- Whose work is most visible in the classroom library?
- Which voices seem to be missing from what is being shared?

- Whose work is most popular in students' independent reading?
- Which genre is popular right now, and how inclusive is that section of the library?

Gaps we've recently found in our classroom libraries include:

- holidays that were not represented in our classroom libraries;
- genres that are not as widely published for the age group we teach;
- nonfiction authors that readers could fall in love with;
- author diversity within a genre; and
- books that show disability and ability in incidental ways.

Curating our libraries is an ongoing process. So, when we notice a gap, we make filling that gap a goal and commitment. We tend to look for resources, and we focus on that gap in our own reading. We are also intentional about spending time and money to fill any gap we discover.

When we found that our poetry collection was not as robust and diverse as we would like, we committed to reading, purchasing, and highlighting more poetry.

A stack of books Franki read one week as she was looking to find more quality graphic novels for her classroom library.

Weeding Your Book Collection Matters

Series books are a huge part of any classroom collection. To organize and weed, Mandy Robek wanted to see all that she had so that she could make intentional decisions as to what to keep and what to weed out.

If we want a well-curated and relevant classroom library, regular weeding matters. We used to keep every book we could get our hands on so that we had a robust classroom library. Although that seemed sensible at the time, we've come to realize that not only did that policy mean we were keeping outdated and irrelevant books on our shelves, but it also had the potential of exposing students to books that were harmful due to negative tropes and stereotypes.

Early in her teaching life, Franki read *The Indian in the Cupboard* to her fourth graders. It was a well-loved read-aloud, and many children went on to read the sequels. But Franki realized years later how problematic this book was and removed every book in the series from her bookshelves. Early on, she had not realized the harm that this book did; but after reading Dr. Debbie Reese's work for years, she realized the negative stereotypes that this book was built upon — the dress of this toy, the way he speaks, the actions. Reading it now, it is hard for her to believe she did not see these problems years ago, but the truth is, she didn't. This book had, in fact, won many awards, and although we rely on reviews and book awards to help us find books, we must rely on experts when reviews have missed the mark on a book.

This book was one that Franki's students loved during her first few years as a fourth-grade teacher. "Because kids love it," however, is no reason to keep a harmful book on our shelves. Once we realize or learn that a book is harmful, we must remove it. We cannot say we are committed to creating strong classroom libraries yet keep such books on our shelves.

Keeping a book in our classroom because we love it is also not a reason to have them take up space on our shelves.

Mandy took time weeding over the summer as she was making room for new books. She had recently changed grade levels, and some of the books were no longer needed in her new classroom. Others were problematic or no longer the best books to include in her collection.

Dr. Laura Jiménez writes about teacher nostalgia in her article "The Overwhelmingly White, Straight, and Able Face of Children's Literature" (2018). She reminds us, "One major issue literary gatekeepers have is the assumption that a book that was good for them is good for all readers. Books written today have racist, homophobic, ableist, sexist representations, so you can bet your sweet bippy that books written 10, 20, 30, 50, and 100 years ago hold miserably racist, ableist, homophobic, sexist depictions."

Franki learned that books she loved as a child were not the books her students would also love. After *From the Mixed-Up Files of Mrs. Basil E. Frankweiler* had been untouched for years, she decided to read it aloud to her new class. However, her fifth graders let her know (loudly) that the story was totally unbelievable because "how were there no cameras in the museum to see the kids sleeping there?"

Our own nostalgia (that we loved it as a child or past classes have enjoyed a book) can get in the way of curating a quality classroom library, if we let it. Books that have harmful stereotypes or tropes are the most important reason we weed books, but there are other reasons and types of books to weed as well, including:

- books that haven't been read by students in a while;
- books that are no longer considered high in quality as compared to others published since that time;
- books purchased because of one class, one student, or one trend that no longer applies;
- books that were popular when we taught another grade level but are not interesting to students in this new grade level;
- books that we purchased because the topic matched a content unit of study but are not interesting to students;
- books that are no longer popular enough and can be accessed in the school library;
- classics that are no longer relevant to our readers;
- books that are falling apart; and
- books we acquired for free or purchased at a bargain price at a garage sale when our library was much smaller, and we don't need "meh" books anymore.

What Counts as Reading?

When we talk about classroom library design, we often only think about the physical classroom library. But there are many types of reading that do not fit into book baskets or on shelves. These include:

- audiobooks
- podcasts
- ebooks
- blogs
- news sites/sports news sites
- digital magazines
- videos

We are committed to making sure that our readers know that all reading is valued in our classrooms, and for these to be valued and seen as part of the classroom library, we must make sure that we amplify them in various ways:

- share an audiobook as a read-aloud instead of the teacher reading the book aloud;
- have devices with audiobooks available;
- share podcasts during mini-lessons;
- project ebook versions of the text during read-aloud or mini-lessons, and use the annotation features to record thinking;
- bookmark sites that have quality content for elementary readers. Include news sites, sports news sites, podcasts, and other digital texts;
- recommend these types of texts rather than only recommending books; and
- embed a variety of digital texts and tools in lessons across the day.

There are several ways to organize digital texts for students. Clare Landrigan, literacy expert in Massachusetts, created Virtual Classroom Libraries and Bookrooms using Padlet, which she generously shared. This is a great resource and a great model for sharing digital texts with elementary readers. We use her idea for curating book collections as well as curating collections of news sites, podcasts, and more.

Audiobooks

We have seen the power of audiobooks for supporting all readers firsthand. Emily, a fifth grader in Franki's room, loved the series The Imaginary Veterinary and was following along with the audiobooks. She completed *The Sasquatch Escape* and

The Lonely Lake Monster, and she was excited to begin the third book in the series, *The Rain Dragon Rescue*, but was disappointed to learn that the book was not available as an audiobook. Franki met with her and listened to her talk about her disappointment.

Then Franki suggested she read this one without the audiobook. Franki explained that after reading two of the books in the series, Emily knew the characters and what to expect from the series. Franki asked if she wanted to try this one without the audio, but Emily let her know that she didn't think she could read the book on her own. Franki knew otherwise. She opened the book and asked Emily to give it a try, and Emily was thrilled to realize that she could, in fact, read the book on her own — and she went on to finish the series.

Audiobooks are wonderful for several reasons. The incredible narrations are often enjoyable, and because of this, many readers prefer audiobooks to paper or electronic books. Audiobooks also let our readers know that reading can happen anywhere, so for readers who get sick when reading in the car, an audiobook is a great answer. For our elementary readers, audiobooks invite readers to engage in stories that might be a bit challenging to read without some support.

Ebooks

We love ebooks, and we know many students do, too! We know the ways they can support readers as well as the ways they can distract readers, so we are mindful about using ebooks in intentional ways. Many ebook readers have a variety of annotation tools. Just as our students have access to sticky notes and highlighters when they are in the classroom, we also want them to have access to and knowledge about using digital annotation tools in their reading.

Read-Alouds

There are also several sites that offer read-alouds of children's books. There are many ways to experience a book, and we want our readers to have a full reading life that includes as many formats as possible.

Searchable Databases

Searchable databases such as PebbleGo are important resources for our readers and writers to have access to. Not only are these great sources for information and reading, but learning to search is a skill we want students to learn to use well.

Blogs and News/Sports News Sites

Every year, Franki has a fifth grader who does not consider themselves a reader but who reads pages and pages of sports news and statistics about their favorite team online daily. Making sure our readers see that this reading "counts" and that they are, in fact, readers is work in itself, but one way we push back against any ambiguity is by making sure this type of reading is valued and "counts" as reading in our classroom. We do this in a variety of ways.

We try to use blog posts and digital news articles/videos in much of our teaching. We want our students to have experience gaining information from several sources; so, we want to have those texts available for independent reading as well. Curating news and sports news sites that are appropriate and interesting for elementary students and then linking those for students as part of our digital classroom library is key.

Public Library Connection

We want our students to have easy access to the public library website, as we know the public library will have a larger selection than we have. We also want to build library habits in our students; being able to access the public library to look for books as well as to access other digital resources is important in children's understanding of all that the public library offers to a reader.

Digital Resources for Finding Books Not in a Classroom Library

We also want to curate safe sites for our readers to discover books we may not have in our classroom library. Linking to child-safe sites like Bookelicious is one way to let children learn about new books and then seek them out in our school or public library.

Common Sense Media has a good list of family-friendly recommended podcasts.

Podcasts and Videos

Podcasts and videos are often overlooked, but audio and visual literacy are important, and so much can be learned through podcasts, video, and other media. When our students are only listening to podcasts and watching videos for entertainment, they don't understand their power for learning. So, we try to embed both video and podcasts into our days. Experiencing these forms of media as learners will help them be more active consumers of the content.

Afterword

By Detra M. Price-Dennis

During my last two years of teaching at an elementary school, I failed to explain why the design of my classroom space, along with the furniture and materials in that space, made a difference in my pedagogy. As I read this book, I really wish I could go back in time with it on my Kindle to offer my school community a chance to think about how classroom spaces reveal our philosophies and beliefs about students without us saying a word. As I think about it, the classroom spaces children are invited to learn in expose why certain students can move from space to space in a building and seem like a completely different learner in each of those spaces. When I was trying to point this out and request different furniture and materials, I believe some people viewed my requests as an unnecessary luxury focused only on the aesthetics of the space. But the truth is, I wanted my students to collaborate, innovate, and ideate, and my classrooms needed to reflect that goal.

If I had this book in my hands back then, I would have known to say, "I am trying to create a learning environment with flexible seating on multiple levels, with large floor pillows, whiteboards, tables that vary in size, and a few desks to encourage students to make decisions about what type of space they need to work in for different types of assignments." I wanted my students to have choices that reflected their needs as a learner. Thanks to Lynsey and Franki, those of you reading this book will not have to face my dilemma because you have everything you need across these pages to make your case.

I spend a lot of time thinking about how to assemble spaces for learning, albeit in virtual settings, but occasionally in face-to-face environments as well. The key ideas from this book are pushing my thinking about how to create spaces for learning that grow with students and reflect their potential as learners. There are so many gems in this book that spoke to me as an educator and researcher who works with a variety of students each week. I have selected my top five to share with you.

1. **Humanizing pedagogies thrive when we realize that classrooms belong to children.**

   At the heart of this book is a question that compels us to grapple with how are we honoring children's humanity.

   How do our decisions about space, pedagogy and creativity get us closer to that vision? The authors invite us to consider what it means to learn from people who prefer a circle instead of a row. Lynsey and Franki are teachers who want to flatten power dynamics and build classroom communities where everyone can shift from teacher to learner depending on their needs, talents, and interests. They are intentional in sharing a vision that pushes against systems of schooling that support linear "banking pedagogies," or that position the teacher as the most knowledgeable and powerful person in the room. Instead, they invite us to imagine classrooms as spaces that are reciprocal and center the needs of students. This type of classroom is only possible when students are thought of during the initial design process and included as co-designers once the school year begins. Humanizing pedagogies seek to create learning environments that build on what is possible.

2. **The classroom environment is the co-teacher.**

If humanizing spaces center the emotional, physical, and intellectual needs of students, then we must consider the role of space as it frames the ecosystem where learning takes place. Another key idea Lynsey and Franki offer us is to set up learning spaces with children. They give us a vivid metaphor to think about when designing spaces with children in mind, such as the classroom as a coffee shop. When I put spaces together for children, I want an Edtech start-up feel. I could name that before reading this book, but after reading this book, I know why.

If you have ever toured or worked in an Edtech space, you can feel the pulse of ideas flowing all around you. There are open spaces and glass white boards with diagrams of new ideas. There are lots of different seating options and ideation spaces where people are talking, writing ideas on charts, and collaborating to create something. There is a lot of doing, so the space feels dynamic. When I walk into a classroom and the space feels stagnant and only the teacher is doing, I know within 60 seconds that I cannot learn in that type of space. This revelation is essential for me to know and offers clarity about how it informs the way I design spaces for learners that reflect my vision.

After reading this book, I am now clear that I must make sure the students I work with have the language and experiences to name the types of environments they need to be their most imaginative and creative selves. What I know for sure is that classroom design for student agency means I need to think of every design choice as a pedagogical team member — from the lighting to the cushions on the floor.

3. **Classroom spaces should captivate and inspire learners.**
Throughout the chapters in this book, Lynsey and Franki ask us to be thoughtful about every item we place in a classroom and lean into the space as part of the curriculum. However, designing a thoughtful and responsive classroom also requires us to make sure the culture in that classroom inspires and encourages students to be their best selves. In the book *Creativity Inc.,* Ed Catmull writes, "A hallmark of a healthy creative culture is that its people feel free to share ideas, opinions, and criticisms."

    I often wonder how children are expected to learn in spaces where their ideas — particularly those that challenge the curriculum — are dismissed or suppressed. This book makes it clear that fostering a culture of learning that values different perspectives, life experiences, and the ideas that blossom from those perspectives and life experiences means that we must make sure learners feel comfortable physically, emotionally, and intellectually. It also calls on us to let go of practices and policies that reflect power dynamics rooted in surveilling and controlling children and shift to practices that engage and inspire them. Connected to this idea is the need to then make sure that classroom spaces support students being able to act on this information in ways that make sense for them as learners.

4. **Technologies are tools that support learners as they consume, curate, create, and disseminate information.**
As teachers, we can show students how we are intentional about the ways we integrate technology in the classroom to support access and agency. This work begins with recognizing students' need for choice and experience with digital tools, apps, and platforms to develop knowledge and fluidity when exploring them. Students should be able to decide what materials and tools they need to make sense of the content they are learning and move across those materials, devices, and platforms in ways that demonstrate their understanding of how the affordances of those tools are connected to the goals they have in mind as learners.

    The authors provide us with clear examples of how we can work with students to create digital anchor charts, annotate texts on a whiteboard, or locate information in ways that are intuitive and accessible. The choices they made as teachers reflect their commitments to center the needs of learners in ways that maximize the choices their students have available to process what they are learning. This approach makes all tools available to students so they can decide what they need.

5. **Keep asking questions that make visible what is getting in the way of student agency and learning.**

The last compelling lesson I will share is to be clear about your purpose and move forward with a vision of how you will address the barriers that get in the way of your classroom being a place where students experience joy and creativity each day. We need clarity about what we have control over and what we do not, along with discernment to channel our energies toward solving the problems we can address, while shining a light on those that require collective action.

Lynsey and Franki could have been satisfied with being great teachers and co-creating spaces with children that felt welcoming. But they kept asking questions, doing deep dives into the literature on the topic, and being reflective about putting what they were learning into place. They were vigilant about noticing when students encountered barriers to their learning, and they did something about it. As I was reading the last chapter, I realized that this work is a journey, not a checklist. It is supposed to feel uncomfortable at times and challenge us to be the teachers our students deserve.

The valuable insights I am reflecting on from this book will inform the work I do with students. Lynsey and Franki made the case for us to center children when designing classroom spaces. Throughout the book, they offer thoughtful examples of how to do this in ways that reflect a commitment to student choice, agency, and shared decision-making. In the near future, I look forward to visiting schools referenced in this book as a catalyst for change.

Index

Authors

Lynsey Burkins has worked for children for the past eighteen years and currently serves third-grade students. She works toward creating antiracist spaces where children feel free, have agency, and know they are loved. She believes books are primary vehicles to help children become freer. She also presents on topics such as using literature to help students make sense of their world and literature as a vehicle to nurture students' spirit and minds. She received her master's degree in language, literacy, and culture from The Ohio State University. She is a member of NCTE and the outgoing national chair of NCTE's Build Your Stack, an initiative that works to build teachers' expertise in knowing and using quality literature in the classroom. You can find her at @lburkins on X, formerly Twitter.

Franki Sibberson is a literacy leader with over thirty years of experience as an elementary classroom teacher in Ohio. Franki served as president of the National Council of Teachers of English. She is the coauthor of several books, including *Beyond Leveled Books*, *Still Learning to Read*, *Day-to-Day Assessment in the Reading Workshop*, and *Digital Reading: What's Essential in Grades 3–8*. She currently serves as the Executive Director of SproutFive's Institute for Professional Learning. Franki also provides leadership and consulting to schools and nonprofits.

This book was typeset in Canvas Inline, Canvas Script, HanziPen SC, KohinoorLatin, and The Salvador Condensed by Cynthia Gomez.

The typefaces used on the cover include Adobe Caslon Pro, Blackbird, Canvas Inline, Cera Pro, and HanziPen TC.

This book was printed on 80 lb. gloss paper.